tHE

book

OF

A

tHOUSAND

eYES

Previous Books By Lyn Hejinian

Poetry

Saga/Circus (Omnidawn, 2008)

Lola (belladonna, 2005)

My Life in the Nineties (Shark Books, 2003)

The Fatalist (Omnidawn, 2003)

On Laughter: A Melodrama (written with Jack Collom; Baksun Books, 2003)

Slowly (Tuumba Press, 2002)

A Border Comedy (Granary Books, 2001)

The Beginner (Spectacular Books, 2000; Tuumba Press, 2002)

Happily (Post-Apollo Press, 2000)

Chartings (written with Ray Di Palma; Chax Press, 2000)

Sunflower (written with Jack Collom; The Figures, 2000)

Sight (written with Leslie Scalapino; Edge Books, 1999)

Wicker (written with Jack Collom; Rodent Press, 1996)

The Little Book of a Thousand Eyes (Smoke-Proof Press, 1996)

Guide, Grammar, Watch, and The Thirty Nights (Australia: Folio, 1996)

The Cold of Poetry (Sun & Moon Press, 1994)

The Cell (Sun & Moon Press, 1992)

The Hunt (Spain: Zasterle Press, 1991)

Oxota: A Short Russian Novel (The Figures, 1991)

Individuals (written with Kit Robinson; Chax Press, 1988)

The Guard (Tuumba Press, 1984)

Redo (Salt-Works Press, 1984)

My Life (Burning Deck, 1980; expanded version Sun & Moon, 1987)

Gesualdo (Tuumba Press, 1978)

Writing is an Aid to Memory (The Figures, 1978; reprinted by Sun & Moon, 1996)

A Mask of Motion (Burning Deck, 1977)

A Thought is the Bride of What Thinking (Tuumba Press, 1976)

CRITICAL PROSE

THE GRAND PIANO: AN EXPERIMENT IN COLLECTIVE AUTOBIOGRAPHY,
(WRITTEN WITH RAE ARMANTROUT, STEVE BENSON, CARLA HARRYMAN, TOM
MANDEL, TED PEARSON, BOB PERELMAN, KIT ROBINSON, RON SILLIMAN, AND
BARRETT WATTEN; MODE A, 2006–2009)
THE LANGUAGE OF INQUIRY (UNIVERSITY OF CALIFORNIA PRESS, 2000)
TWO STEIN TALKS (WEASELSLEEVES PRESS, 1995)
LENINGRAD (WRITTEN WITH MICHAEL DAVIDSON, RON SILLIMAN, BARRETT
WATTEN; MERCURY HOUSE, 1991)

THE
book
OF
A
thousand
eyes

Lyn Hejinian

OMNIDAWN PUBLISHING
RICHMOND, CALIFORNIA
2012

Cover art by Chaffee Earl Hall Jr, "untitled collage," 1967.
Courtesy of Lyn Hejinian

Book cover and interior design by Cassandra Smith

INITIATIVE

Omnidawn Publishing is committed to preserving ancient
forests and natural resources. We elected to print this title on
30% postconsumer recycled paper, processed chlorine-free. As
a result, for this printing, we have saved:

9 Trees (40' tall and 6-8" diameter)
4,067 Gallons of Wastewater
4 million BTUs of Total Energy
258 Pounds of Solid Waste
902 Pounds of Greenhouse Gases

Omnidawn Publishing made this paper choice because our
printer, Thomson-Shore, Inc., is a member of Green Press
Initiative, a nonprofit program dedicated to supporting authors,
publishers, and suppliers in their efforts to reduce their use of
fiber obtained from endangered forests.

For more information, visit www.greenpressinitiative.org

Environmental impact estimates were made using the Environmental Defense
Paper Calculator. For more information visit: www.edf.org/papercalculator

Library of Congress Cataloging-in-Publication Data

Hejinian, Lyn.
The book of a thousand eyes / Lyn Hejinian.
  p. cm.
ISBN 978-1-890650-57-5 (trade pbk. : alk. paper)
I. Title.
PS3558.E4735B66 2012
811'.54--dc23

                    2011051411

Published by Omnidawn Publishing, Richmond, California
www.omnidawn.com   (510) 237-5472   (800) 792-4957
10 9 8 7 6 5 4 3 2 1
ISBN: 978-1-890650-57-5

Acknowledgements

Versions of some of these poems have appeared in various literary magazines. These include (in alphabetical order): *Abraham Lincoln, Aerial, Amit, Antithesis, Berkeley Poetry Review, Black Bread, Black Warrior Review, Bombay Gin, DWB* (in Dutch), *Calliope, Coconut, Colorado Review, Conjunctions, Court Green, Dirty, Fluid, Fulcrum, Grand Street, Green Zero, Hambone, Hot Bird Mfg, NO: A Journal of the Arts, ParaSpheres 2, Parthenon West Review, Plan B, Proliferations, Rattapallax, Southern Review* (Perth, Australia), *Try, Volt, Xconnect, Zoland Poetry*

Some of the poems, most in earlier versions, were included in recent anthologies, including:

Bay Area Poetries, Stephanie Young, ed. (Faux Press, 2006)
The Best American Poetry 2005, Paul Muldoon, ed. (Scribner's, 2006)

50: A Celebration of Sun & Moon Classics, Douglas Messerli, ed. (Sun & Moon Press, 1995)

Ghosting Atoms: Poems and Reflections Sixty Years After the Bomb, Olivia Friedman and Lyn Hejinian, eds (UC Regents and Consortium for the Arts, 2007)

Broadside versions of several of the poems have been printed in limited editions:

The poem beginning "Some people are meant to sleep in clover" was published as a Small Press Traffic broadside

The poem beginning "History has compass, time speeds past, memory gets lost" was published as a broadside and distributed at a conference on "Poetry and Public Language" (University of Plymouth, UK, 2007)

The poem beginning "There in your hand is an emerald hoe" was published as a Naropa / Smokeproof Press broadside

The poem beginning "To achieve reality (where objects thrive on people's passions)" was published as a broadside at Lewis and Clark College

The author thanks the editors of these publications for their support and care.

Dedications

The following poems first appeared as part of a mixed media collaboration titled "The Eye of Enduring" that the painter Diane Andrews Hall and I created; they were exhibited at the Sherrill Haines Gallery (San Francisco, 1995); all of these poems are dedicated to Diane:

"When I speak it's clear that I don't reject" (a copy, silkscreened on glass, is in the
        collection of the University of California, Berkeley Art Museum)
"Visibility has made waking good"
"This comes after a feeling of vigorous apathy, the joy of being"
"The height of the grass along the path through the field increases at every telling"
"A stream of particulars, a stream of abstractions, and wicked geese"
"I'd attributed entirety to the cattle"
"Passion itself is not repetitious but it can result"
"Philosophy should not be hostile to the eyes"

Individual poems (indicated here by first lines or title) are dedicated as follows:

"A Fable" is for Carla Harryman
"Everyday I cannot bring myself the wildlife of the wilderness" is for Jack Collom
"I am writing now in preconceptions" is for John Zorn, after his Elegy
"I might perhaps have been inclined to call a dream an expectation" is dedicated to
        the memory of Alexei Parshchikov
"My sleep has reasoned miniscule" was written in memory of Jerry Estrin
"Suddenly a film" is for Pierre Alferi
"The lamb butts its head against the udder" is for Brian Whitener
"There in your hand is an emerald hoe" is dedicated to the memory of Charlotte
        Ellertson
"This tale like many others" is dedicated to Lilian and Rosa Ackley, who were there
        when the events happened
"Those who speak about us today—how long will they talk" is for Michael McClure
"Today is 'a day just like any other'" is for Jen Hofer
"We are all being good sports, we are all disappointed" is for Dolores Dorantes
"What is this turbulent moment from which I can't detach myself" is for T. J. Clark

Notes

In the poem beginning "I am having difficulty staying asleep," the quoted line ("Sleep arms us with a terrible freedom") is from Ralph Waldo Emerson.

The opening first line and a half of the poem beginning "When we want something we have to reckon / With probabilities" is quoted from Jean-Paul Sartre, *Existentialism and Human Emotions* (NY: Philosophical Library, Inc, no date), 29.

In the poem beginning "Life must learn history quickly," the lines "But a person is not a sausage as some would have it / Endowed with reason but rather a passion" are adapted from Joakim Garff, *Søren Kierkegaard: A Biography* (Princeton, NJ: Princeton University Press, 2005), 320: "man is not (in Grundtvig's words) a 'sausage endowed with reason' but rather (in Kierkegaard's words) 'passion.'"

In the poem beginning "Surely the sea for the deer browsing…," lines 34-48 are drawn in part from H.G. Wells, "The Time Machine," quoted in Oliver Sacks, "Speed: Aberrations of time and movement," *The New Yorker*, August 23, 2004, 60.

The poem beginning "I am a tattered apology. I have two eyebrows" is drawn from an unpublished short story by Finnian Hurtado.

In the poem beginning "Temptations thronging through my hours are strong," lines 14-18 are drawn in part from H.G. Wells, "The Time Machine" and "The New Accelerator," both quoted in Oliver Sacks, "Speed: Aberrations of time and movement," *The New Yorker*, August 23, 2004, 60

IN HOMAGE
TO SCHEHERAZADE

❋

AND

FOR
MARKA AND AMITY, FINNIAN AND DIEGO

The night has a thousand eyes,
  And the day but one

Francis William Bourdillon (1852-1921)

✻

                              I'll write
and I myself can read
to see if what I've written is right.
Sleep offers an excuse
                    for substitution.

But who else would dream
             the world one thinks?
It's only there
            the world repeats.

Many days are often mine.
Do I feel that
            timeless satisfaction?
It's seldom said.

                    Who can be trusted?
                      One tells
        but cannot recognize.

✼

Reposed, inclined, allowed
and nightly liking place
a person rested for ...

                              Does it matter?
in antagonism, in sleep?

For love
the fingers closed
                    For recovery
and place

with oblivion arrested...

✳

The bed is made of sentences which present themselves as what they are
Some soft, some hardly logical, some broken off
Sentences granting freedom to memories and sights

Then is freedom about love?
Bare, and clumsily impossible?
Our tendernesses give us sentences about our mistakes
Our sentiments go on as described
The ones that answer when we ask someone who has mumbled to say what
        he or she has said again
In bed I said I liked the flowing of the air in the cold of night
Such sentences are made to aid the senses

Tonight itself will be made—it's already getting dark
I'm not afraid to look nor afraid to be seen in the dark
Is there a spectral sentence? a spectator one?
Is it autobiographical?
No—the yearning inherent in the use of any sentence makes it mean far more
        than "we are here"

Because we are not innocent of our sentences we go to bed
The bed shows with utter clarity how sentences in saying something make
        something
Sentences in bed are not describers, they are instigators

❀

I slept but the poise was pitching
We were all dining in a tree
We were dream natives
We were aroused
A sensation seized me during that time of something meaningless and
        unexpected, a sensation of the unusual spell cast by everything on
        earth without exception
I knew I couldn't help but miss some things in life
But I shouldn't do so in sleep by making my own decisions
Anything could come to me   .
Sleep itself
I could be defenseless—satiated, metamorphosed, pitched
Time itself would provide an uprising—of interests and alterations and
        defenses
So time is dream
And we can be switched
Sleep might be the other on which my eyes are fixed
And even now I can't relinquish my sensation of that something persistent,
        my recalcitrant great pleasure in feeling both the passage and the
        fullness of time

✻

Then the fourth night began. Through the open window I heard the falsetto of a singing man. One of the triplets couldn't sleep and brought me a book to read. She sat on my lap.

I opened the book.

Once (I began) ....

Why singing threatened a singing man

Once a girl became a nightingale just as the drifting light on that particular late afternoon was turning purple under enormous winter clouds. A moment later a storm began. A dazzling murky wind shattered the shadows of the trees.

Is it true that men sing for themselves and not for others? the nightingale girl asked no one and nothing in particular. She had always wondered whether birds were miserable in stormy weather and she was discovering that they were not. She wanted to communicate this information. I have very little to say to myself, she said, and the sound of her voice trembled in the air. The rain swirled like silt in a racing tide refusing to settle.

> bird
> of music word
> in a well again
> well
> word aloud

Birds nest in their omnipotent meditations. What but these are the contents of mature development?

A fugitive was running from shadow to shadow below, afraid of...

But no story should speak only of the past. We sing to be ourselves tomorrow, the fugitive said to no one or nothing in particular.

There was no answering sound.

O, he said to himself in the silence of his thoughts, O, inflexible nightmare! I've been doomed to silence!

> dawns descend
> on dawns
> in darks
> from tree to tree

✳

A terrible attention is given by night
I've been presented to it short—or long if the night is short
My sentence is garbling grammar to the inside as phenomena change
       concentration

The breeze is sweet, the window blows open, I go to bed
I might have gone rather to a different bed in order to change the order of
       events
Hours of necessity and sense

But a natural blindness afflicts me with questions, those sentimental
       postulations:
              is it time?
              is this going to be enough?
              is the work well-done and done?
              why are we so angry?
That last is the most sentimental—we know why we are angry
We know why we uncurl as in a tragicomedy waggling a foot,
       proposing distractions, and then raging at social imposition and
       our inability to concentrate

Logic, logic—that's the substance of the shift
That instrument of attention, that common cause of transformation
A different experience and a different occasion are inevitable and occur the
       very next night

✳

To remember a dream is to realize that one was
I do, as I awake, experience the becoming conscious of something unconscious
        in the night—to the extent that it's possible to be so, unconscious
        throughout, but almost speaking, as a fortune-teller might, with a
        fortune-teller's hindsight
Accurate prophesying solely requires interpreting what has already occurred,
        since the future, like fortune, is to be found not in events but in their
        meanings
The future is fortune's form
But it lacks familiarity, the criterion for belief
But it is real by definition, being unaffected by what we think of it
It is regardless of our sense of metallic clatter, our sense of a glint of lemon
        yellow, our sense of pressing, horror, pleasure, flight, etc.
It is regardless of the future
So the future seems a definite conclusion
But that's not accurate

The future is an accuracy requiring patience, presence
We can't predict if we don't watch
Watching makes what comes to be watched
The future requires requiring
It needs microphone and cold and exaggeration tossing
The sub-zero
Foreigners
Excess, hum, buckets of dream-blue lassitude that only an angel would see as
        action

✻

There was once an angel who had a neighbor, and this neighbor was ambitious. He wanted more than money or fame, he said; he wanted immortality.

"Why's that?" asked the angel.

The angel had lived an unnaturally long time, but nonetheless he understood some things about nature, and here at the end of a long summer day, he was watering the small garden in front of his house.

"Well," said the neighbor, somewhat portentously but also tentatively—he was a sensitive person but he'd considered this for a long time and he now felt that his thoughts were correct and important—"I don't want my feelings, so very dear and strong and uniquely arising from my life, to go suddenly unfelt, as they will be, when I'm dead."

"So you think you want to be immortal."

"Yes."

"But," said the angel, "it is precisely the immortals who are dead."

Moral: Certain experienced continuums—for example, time, space, the ego—are bridges but without chasms.

Moral: Even when an angel makes you fly, you are the wings.

Moral: An angel's pugnacious twaddle may be as irrefutable as a pistol and in the same way wrong.

Moral: It's not the length of a life but the tension of its parts that lets resound all that it feels.

✻

The first hour of this arrangement of thought objects is deathlike
Then as sleep encounters nature it attracts pensive wandering
The westward-moving "I" follows the sun but so slowly it loses ground

"I" dream of telling a man to be precise
I want him to discern the ideological form and function of the terms
         "barbarian," "local watering hole," and "women"
I wake, turn, think of turning, widen, until dehumanized I'm something
         congenial in brain beyond control
The gap between world and mind is sleepable
The concept of "same time" serves as an invitation to attend while things
         assimilate, mutate, or aesthetically vacillate

Just as the second hour meets the first I dream an explanation but the
         explanation ramifies
I extrapolate and that's conditional
There is nothing unconditional—there is always room
It spreads like the shadow of knowledge over a sleeping person
Immortal before, immortal after, but mortal now

✻

Just after dusk of a plum blue night between the sixth and seventh days, under a distant, uncommunicative, stubborn or perhaps passive but intimidating, blank (celestial) sky, the wind unpredictably (it seemed to the observer, who was increasingly reflective about this life) began, with dappling effect on all the surfaces that the observer regarded as reality, to blow.

But the word *suddenly* is always relative.

As far as the observer was concerned, at least for the moment (which was reflected on the windowpane), nothing was irrelevant, and in saying so, the observer didn't care who understood; the moment could not be stopped and was therefore not a vivid terminus of experience.

I am not the dupe of dreamlands of conclusion, the observer said (one should deny everything attributed to it). All I want—though I'm only guessing—is to watch the flicker, twinkle, waggle (the instincts are not always blind, nor are they always invariable), and flow of transformation (however delicately modulated)—and then to swim in it. It, said the observer, is endless—infinite—nothing.

And if the observer hadn't been watching, with repetitions embracing every expectation, then later, for an instant, the observer would never have seen that nothing had changed.

❃

Sleep constitutes experience
delivered. But that might be music.
Or lies. Association is clearly
the best means for shifting
to a waking world with its status
of law and assonance. Each sleep
is an apple in a metonymic world then
and waking remains recurrent. It gives us
the memory that *this* activity requires,
a broken sequence of second recognitions
which slipping by become themselves.

✳

One sleeps and is doing out of deeds
I dream that I am conscious but not that I participate
Yet the thing has gradually grown visible even to dull eyes
Yet eyes none am

✳

Then the singing man, whose doom had yet to come, spoke. "Darkness,
      we are two and therefore I am two."
But the darkness would not revert to its ordinary shape. Instead, just as
      the man tried to close his mouth, the nightingale flew out.
"Beautiful man," it said, "enjoy all the power of your sex, and I will enjoy
      the secrets of mine."
They agreed to this plan.
A hunter who had finished his lunch only moments before came into the
      forest.
He fell into a daydream which was fatal to him.

Poetry may be didactic; it is certain that it's the best place to mix genres.
This may be because narrative expectations....
Well—imagine a narrative expecter, out in a forest at dawn. It shouldn't
      be taken for a forest ranger. Forest rangers are explainers and law
      enforcers, but the narrative expecter is a hunter.
The narrative expecter may also be an animal, the object of the hunt.
Folktales, by definition, exist in many versions.
For example, the "hunter" who comes into the forest in this story is, in
      one version, a "cop."
But here that would have been all wrong. Here, the narrative expecter is
      like a marvelous centaur.

✳

I am writing now in preconceptions
Those of sex and ropes
Many frantic cruelties occur to the flesh of the imagination
And the imagination does have flesh to destroy
And the flesh has imagination to sever
The mouth is just a body filled with imagination
Can you imagine its contents—the dripping into a bucket
And its acts—the ellipses and chaining apart
The feather
The observer

The imagination, bare, has nothing to confirm it
There's just the singing of the birds
The sounds of the natural scream
The imagination wishes to be embraced by freedom
It is laid bare in order to be desired
But the imagination must keep track of the flesh responding—its
        increments of awareness—a slow progression
It must be beautiful and it can't be free

✿

Now, you've exposed your arms
You've stiffened your neck
You are snuffling
You are lying hot in the wet night air by the open window
On this nineteenth night, with the rain now falling and the branches of
      a tree knocking against the wall, the sound of the tires of an
      accelerating bus splatters the silence
You are suddenly awake and shaking with fear

Slowly though suddenly you are realizing that all these recognitions are
      from a *past* life, one that wasn't awful in itself but is awful now in
      having been
You are dead
You are hot not with life but with fright
It seems that being dead doesn't exclude you
On the other hand, your being dead doesn't exclude your being alive,
      either

You feel the inappropriately blue fabric of the blanket in the close night
      like an animal against your arm in the middle of the bed
You'd rather risk the very edge where the sheets are smooth
You experience pulsations of unconsciousness—spasms of oblivion
      followed by involuntary recuperative mental balancings
I?
You?
Living demands sustained temptations

Awake, unconsciousness remains—but like a fingerprint
Life is an antecedent, and an inevitability, but of what?

＊

then this emotion
        will come to view
under two yellow eyes
        two dark birds

✳

We have come on our own and we'll stay
But let's demand something now to know of where we are
Knowledge is embodied—and the body is trembling, terrified because it's
        unprepared
It forgot to get ready, it forgot to pack, it forgot to read

As a result of not testing the real for activity we begin to wonder who
        lives
So tomorrow I will torture myself
All that is ordinary will be illegitimate
This will be the consummation of all that is going to sadden

I am not saying that personal generosity will solve everything—a person
        can't even solve today by midnight
Generosity cannot bury anonymity
It cannot even take itself as animal
To believe it to be what we truly believe it to be we must open it

The segments of life taken in separation and laid side by side
Cruelty is always turning kindly aside
It creates a clinical situation—I, a body, turning for speculation

But love exalts only truths that are undemonstrable
They turn true by demanding some activity
So I will say "I" and remain

❋

Some people are meant to sleep in clover
These must be sleep specific people
Some toss in bed
There are varieties of rest as there are of flesh and power
But poetry is so precise that each word must be singular
And then some two are plural
In time, in transformation, in fortune
The logics left out shouldn't serve as interruptions
They might be filled with anything
Nocturnal plenitudes of focus
Logics are like constellations
A thing itself when it's full of its own interpretation
And since you can't stop there, some people are logical to dream in perfect
        flowers

✳

I might perhaps have been inclined to call a dream an expectation
There's very little separation of the outer world from the one within
I say I have the urge to bite you
I am an animal
I'm afraid of what other people think and my worries lead to
dishevelments
I no sooner fall on A than I anticipate B and get ready
Each shape I am, I feel, potentially
I'm even afraid of what I might think
I'm afraid of the shapes the thoughts may take, the evidences as they form
Things found in their postponements
In a throng of things dreamed there are always delays
I wake myself
Promises exist inside of time, time is unwavering in its usefulness
I am seized—justice is not always blind

❀

The sadness! the injustice!
It's true I want to know, I want to look
But what is it?

✳

Sleep requires a lot of space
The justice and autonomy of one

Here's a nocturnal discovery
Asleep we are carnally irate

Our sleep has no conclusion
Our sleep is made of words

The library of decisions is the mind
Then we dream to become encyclopedic

A sky of words and words of plains
A heaven of grounds and preparation

The thoroughness of sleep is great
It is enthusiastic, austere, and strong

It is stranger than habit and than obsession
Sleep is as abundant as the world is incomplete

There is sleep always to recognize
One sleep is a rolling burial

Another a badger's hole
Or something arithmetical, the rhythm between sounds

Or a judgment that is made
A place, inordinate or blank

And then another place added
To increase the consequence, that everything exists

❀

One night I loved the night continuously with tension and watched television
Infinity often intercedes
Marxist as teammates, feminist as saints, individuals are given new names
Mine was Martha
Then Gilbert, then Bobby, then Jane, then Pilar
And so on
What a line
I told Timothy to consider *feminist* as analogous to *geologist*
As a geologist knows rocks and soils so a feminist knows power and its spoils
A *feminist*, I said, is like a *botanist* and has a certain expertise
It made sense
It got real
When you're asleep you often think you're still awake
The perfect voice of the wind across the sill says moderately wheeze with
        reason
Illness—that's no metaphor
I'm alerted: illness is no camouflage nor is wealth truth
The skateboarders in the ad which consumes the gist of the show flip
A fountain is shot, then thistles by the wayside
Thistles never oblige

✻

O no, here comes

O boy

O ho

O my god

Okay

Off we go

✻

The night will change
as I strive to depict precisely
to avoid the light since
to understand what
I can't explain
I want to attribute a cause to it
which is to say a change to it

Every passion is
an eccentricity emitting detail ecstatically
irregularly to mind again—
the neck, the knob,
the hub and ram
and rise precisely—to avoid
avoiding the light

The night though
lit is not complete when gone at dawn with the details
it keeps despite the sound of this
awake deliberately and willing
to wait to try for the light it keeps

❀

It is thus, he says, and falls
Here I am and this is what I am
And I am over here
And in the language of the rhinoceros I am this
What am I?

✿

One night I have a dream that is so busy it precludes all creative ideas
I'm furious at myself

I wish I had remembered to project images from it onto a strip of paper
I have gone with a man to get a dachshund, which he insists won't get
          underfoot since he has trained it to stay in the woods collecting
          berries

I know this because the film on which my memories are recorded is in
          black and white
Meanwhile, outside, a street crew is digging up the sidewalk and making
          a terrible din and I'm feeling increasingly enraged

We all need a little getaway spot just to assimilate everything and find out
          what we know
I seize one of the construction workers and point to a window of a house
          across the street, shouting, the woman who lives there is dying

I'm furious at myself
Everyone knows I'm in love with the baseball player named Eugene, but
          I pretend not to know this, and when everyone is about to shout,
          I shout too—"Hey, you bum, you fart harder than you hit"—but
          I'm the only one shouting and Eugene looks at me sadly

I leave this situation unresolved and go up an escalator
Three men are handcuffed to chairs and I hurry to release them—their
          handcuffs are made of wood and shaped like ox-yokes

This is a gesture of defiance—I know that I'm a very good rock and roll
          drummer

A spy who resembles Ingrid Bergman is married to one of the prisoners,
          and she asks me to help her escape with him

Instead when someone telephones we just pass the phone receiver back
    and forth in front of the TV and radio
The joke catches us in a display of outrageous self-indulgence

One of the men insists that the bed has its place in this feud
I say, Excuse me, I want to change position

I'm an old woman but I know people expect more than that
Maybe I should just keep my mouth shut and leave my false teeth in
    permanently

I am afraid of being smothered between the breasts of the scientists
The lecturer has announced that he will speak on the topic of "Pragmatic
    Omniscience"

Once the lecture is underway, there can be no thrashing about
Sport, says the lecturer, is dependent on the occasional appearance of
    wild animals

He presents a slide of a dachshund digging up buried bird bones
This is not a common duck hunter

I say to the host, All now is in the waiting
I worry that my choice of words is somehow suggestive and say, You're
    being insensitive

I feel a strong sense of duty
Alternative sequences are possible, but I don't know how to trigger the
    mechanisms for setting them in motion are locked

❄

Sleeps
are in serial
theory

and the prime
requisite
is to apply them

to the darkening
below zero

✻

The Devil and the Mortal

There was once (and quite recently, so there still may be) a devil who
      went about stiffly in old clothes and prided himself on his lack of
      vanity (which, one might argue, was itself a bit of vanity—but
      then again, as we all learn in time, devils have numerous faults).
This was a contemplative devil, and, though he looked like a man who,
      having bitten off a piece of bread, would make certain to chew
      it for a very long time, he was compassionate and sometimes
      even generous.
When he walked he bobbed his head, communicating glum greetings and
      pessimistic affirmations. His neighbors enjoyed chatting with
      him about the world's bad news.
In the evenings, when the devil was alone, he would sit in readiness, rigid,
      as if in pain, seeming somehow martyred—and perhaps he was
      a martyr, to the burden of his thoughts or to the web of plots
      into which more and more parts of the world are perennially
      being drawn (though without diminishing the world to any
      perceptible degree), though by what it is often hard to say—and
      if one does say, few will listen, agree, or care.
Life is life, is what they say.
This devil was not the only one in the world—according to a certain
      authority, "a mathematical genius," long ago out of a hole in the
      ground, in a single stunning exodus, near Ultima Thule, 2
      trillion, 665 billion, 866 million, 746 thousand, 664 devils
      emerged, not immortal perhaps but so long-lived that the
      distinction between mortal and immortal has been, in their case,
      almost impossible to make.
And this was precisely our particular devil's problem—the distinction
      between life and death.

But why make such a distinction?

✳

Octave!

Allegro!

Nonetheless!

Sleep credulity frenzied cannot distract

Aristotle acts

Pudding orbs and trees in balance come to credulity

Whispered credulity

Conflict in credulity

Contrast in credulity

It takes credulity to grasp at a varied something

Credulity in the same direction

Credulity becoming more by comparison

Credit credulity

Clutter credulity

Credulity we counter with credulity freely

The credulity of the clown in a mishap merry miserably

The credulity of the populace umbrellaed in the rain

The credulity of the conscious mind binds it to its intuitions

The credulous proceed

Credibility accrues to the singer who knows the words to her song

The horse pulling the cart was not credulous, the dog following it was
        intentionally

Things invite credulity

Events demand credulity

Credulity in yonder mountain forms correctly

Belief goes under

Credulity overcomes three girls playing hopscotch temporarily

Leaping credulity leaps *with* credulity

Stretching credulity

Continuing credulity

Insufferable leaping credulity thumps

Suddenly!

Reverse credulity

The credulous must sudden, sink, or circus

The credulous come from credulity and arrive late askew

Then half from that they proceed

Half again from that some thriving carts shrink as they approach

The thriving carts stop to let rules off

On!

Tossing credulity, we live vaguely to include complications

Others are never explained

Picnicking with inexplicable credulity, we sit in the shade and form a
          massive figure

We shift and form another

With credulity provided, we tag walls

Remember credulity in darkness, task at hand

Take credulity for gravity

Lacking credulity I pull my tongue

Gaining credulity I rise to speak

I scrawl graffiti on the wall and sign one "Zola," one "Waghead," one
          "Banquet," one "Vote," and one "Honky Bitch of the
          Bamboozledoisie"

Everything gives off signs of credible life

The credulous are easy to tease

We seat ourselves comfortably one by one and are recognized

Logic goes right out the door, doubt having left it open

Ambivalence can't determine the heights to which we'll climb

An incredible saga

Credulity is incomplete

Why not believe big bodies!

Why not ride wild horses!

There is no superfluous credulity among us

Credulity is rarely indifferent

Viva!

Light, light, thick light down the middle and around the sides sets off
   credulity

Thus the bronze equestrian

Shrink credulity or shimmy it

Calendar credulity or cost it

Come, singer, and prove the song

Credulity recedes to the background

Credulity returns as a result

Credulity in motion encompassing credulity

Let's just hope that farm animals stay more credible than military figures
   in a field

Thus the bronze equestrian

Stravinsky, what a genius!

See circus and believe it!

Can we

Indeed

Personal credulity

Credited credulity

Credulity slips into the cot

We can chronicle credulity

An incredible drama

January through October we confess credulity

The moonlight is critical

✺

One hears music and outcries
which no one else hears
in this voluntary solitude
consuming thousands of sights

And sleep which so much helps
breaks out into events
in moments to spend everything,
each thing as it might be

✻

One day I wake and I'm sick of virtuosity, it makes me spit.

Virtuosos have lost their credibility with me. They're quick but they spin around a slick pole.

Practicing sleight of hand is dishonest work, there's no need for it. Its values are trumped up, and all the while the anxiety it pretends to distract us from is precisely what it activates.

Pretending to be timeless, virtuosity taunts us. It's about fast power, and loneliness—about the lack of good company. It's a bad dream. That's how it draws us in—and that's what it draws us into.

✻

A Fable

A magnificent traveling owl stood on a fine long branch in an orchard
overlooking a long quiet bay or perhaps a sluggish but bright
(because hardly moving and therefore unmuddied) expanse of
a river over a wide sandy shallow bed. The owl turned its head
toward a heavy yellow peach hanging from a twig nearby and
acknowledged its transformation from what it had been before.
"Yeah, well," said the peach modestly. "you know—the days go by."
Suddenly the owl (do you imagine it as a male? a female? and the peach?)
heard a scrap of melody in the breeze, rotund but particular,
almost adolescent and throaty...
But the term "suddenly," as applied to the experience of an owl, should
always suggest patient speculation, extended contemplation,
prolonged acknowledgment, and then peace.
Some ants were passing over the owl's claw.
"I've already been tattooed," said the owl.
The peach—rosy, obscure, and banal—fell.

First Moral: All one should ask of anything else is that it try to do its best.

Second Moral: Instinctively we assume a relationship and judge its
significance when we make a combination of two things.

Third Moral: A mere bare fraud is just what our Western common sense
will never believe the phenomenal world to be.

Fourth Moral: Various women writers will take up the philosophical
quest for uncertainty.

✳

Some days arrive like ships to a beach
with the products of sleep, some are made
conspicuous by insomnia that the imagination keeps
amoral. Grandiose and suspect comparisons
come to all, and it's not just from excitement
as in a bed, some long green shelter, male vs. female,
that we make our transitions, swooping and leaping
from blue ants to broken cups that cellists throw
from the sliding shores of the unyielding sea
in an historical period we can't divorce from life.
With ponderous sincerity we jealously combine
details wistfully disguising our inability to tell
friend from enemy with seemingly altruistic work
and a demeanor we hope is dignified
in order to dream and make room
for our thoughts—thoughts which are elusive
however persistently sleep provides
them, trying to resolve the incongruities that cut them
short and waken us, male with female.

❋

The fingers leave their owls in a calm
Sleep figures the features

Sleep speaks for the bird, the animal
For the round and the residual

Sleep soaks from experience
But why and what?

✻

the fact is made
    with face embedded

dreams remake

    the minimum

        for which there's place

❄

But the worst of speaking in the dark is that the sounds we emit are strange and hollow.

✻

I sat in a stiff-backed chair in the slow parade
intending to overcome my society, overcome myself
good lord, I looked and saw a spider on the clarinet
for it is I who is unnatural
the lower body calmer than the upper
saying "that's the last time I'll send you out for milk"
with tears in my pupils only, the rest of my eyes dry
overlooking the chimney pots of Paris, the rooftop water barrels of
        Manhattan
and sometimes life makes its own books
a tragic presentation of seriously the most trivial comedy's fate
to chain the senseless monster in its bed to a few tugs pulling a blank
        statement
through local news of storms and diminishing sea life
as the spectators' eager mirth vanishes
in the actor's forced laughter
whose echo returns and denounces art
with the stubbornly purposive expertise of a surgeon or over-eager clown
and passed out ice-water to everybody down there
as one apple among many or as a bee among bees

✽

Sleep is only a careless term
Its sensations are between
Its lives are loose and separately apparent
We have no dreams of imitations promised
We go one thousand sleeps to the pole
These we slip between

The traveler has bags, the horse a fence to lean on, the ship a passage north
In a symbolic tale the ship would be a link
But nothing real is typical
In a blink of the eye it becomes a sheep

✻

I want to wake with the thought in its slips
I wonder if it can be taught and lie awake to think
I see that consciously I slide

We're unintentionally equipped to dream
Our thoughts go around our figures
They hold us predicting nothing though they recur

✳

Ooooh, oooooh, ooooh, says the voice of a girl:

I've been attacked by owls,
by owls with towels,
I've been attacked
by snakes with rakes.

                        It is just this kind of ridiculous language, banal
but lacking even banality's pretense at relevance and sense, that I hear in
my sleep; I wake, feeling irritable and depressed.

✻

The sun in fables often speaks
It says, Arise, you reprobate, and stride
The reprobate hides

What is a reprobate
It's accused—and guilty—but of what
The biographer no longer bothers to remind the reprobate to keep her
    sense in the shadows between her words
The guilty must be kept to the subject at hand

Biography belongs both to the sun and to the reprobate but very
    differently
The reprobate went out at last on October the 5th
What year was that
Accusation to the reprobate is tedious, the prolongation of something
    that can never be deferred

All reference to the sun, meanwhile, is blinding
The sun brings out the trucks, the pedestrians, the dogs
In one fable the sun challenges a bus to a race
They are both headed West
In another fable the sun is frozen in the ice and only the flowing blood of
    a wounded creature can release it

From the sun's point of view it casts a shadow on the far side of the
    reprobate which the reprobate regards as her own shadow
From the reprobate's point of view shadows provide shelter from the sun
The sun and the reprobate cannot disagree, their perspectives are
    incommensurable, but if they could they would disagree over
    effects, not causes
The formidable, the dreadful, and the ideal are causes unaffected by the
    sun

＊

My sleep has reasoned miniscule
All is possible
Sleep's reason is neutral

Sleep waits with the waiting questions—
    "you will be a small sign?"
    "a Rembrandt?"
    "is to show oneself all that meaning is?"
This should mean that we continue what we are

We can't imagine all the minute emptinesses (innocences)
Nature is not yet God's book
But increments of our own (reasons) move us
They turn us away, return us
The horizons themselves are made of all such increments
Vague precisions—dissimilars—desires

A single day would be irrational
And we cannot withdraw from reason
When we do something we place reason within it
Having been we are what is

✻

But
I'm of a mule age, I dare like a log.
I live where I live, and I'll bulk graciously

—to zero.

*

I dream—a blameless personal crisis
Even I am gone

The laws can't be enforced
The emotions are lacking

How do I resolve this
I say, be a philosopher today and tomorrow be tired

A policeman arrives and states that he'll remain on one condition
He must bare his right arm

There it is, ma'am, a real flower
My god, I say, to be troubled by such a vivid yellow means something
        unforeseen is going to happen

I'll wake one day of free will, of fidelity
I'll present a fluid demonstration of logic

The panorama of logic, I'll say, requires uninterrupted scanning in sleep
There can be no other foreground than what appears

I reach the beach and the word for it is plague
The sea can speak but its speech is cut off before it can begin

Then I see two vague figures and a man with a fighting mustache and I
        call to them, "Gypsies, gypsies!"
The gypsy has lost his right boot—he is hopping on his left foot with his
        naked right foot wagging in the air

But I've wasted my sympathy—the nakedness of the foot is only an illusion
     prompted by the color of the gypsy's leather boots, so-called
     "natural"
I see a rider just as his horse bucks him off

The ride is very slow, and the rider is recognized by the skill with which he
     has taken the ride, competing for the prize which is a trombone
The dream is brightly lit but it lacks background

Without background there can't be any light source
Everyone who steps back to catch the flying trombone disappears behind
     rocks at the end of the beach

A famous astronaut, whose name is Anton Erst, appears—he cannot hide his
     past forever
Anton Erst squats to await his fellow astronauts, but he is sitting in the path
     of an orange and white wave

I sense that I should have seen this coming
Perhaps I'm not yet ready for an encounter

It's not with my permission that dreams embed knowledge
In the end, I'll win—I'll proclaim that I can't remember all of them

In the line at the ice cream stand, Anton Erst becomes anonymous
From sheer joy we run along the sand, a whole crowd, and I am in front

External stimuli are necessary for the restorative processes
I insist that we go on—I won't listen to any excuse

❋

the day's drawn thrown to song melodic loves we've done

❄

You've taken off your socks, and now your pants, the heavy jeans, they are falling, some coins roll from a pocket, the belt buckle bangs against the floor. You will leave your underpants for me to remove, your shirt is off, the moment is opening, there is no ... I cannot gently remove your underpants, you must gently remove my underpants.

❋

Dreams don't provide the thrill of sleep
Waking does
Sleep only exists in memory
It's imaginary
I can sleep my sleep but I can't observe it
I often feel that I've earned—deserved—it and I'm crazed when it's disturbed
And with all this dreamy word play, I wish I could preserve it
And with it its dreams

I'd dream an honest sleep
I'd dream of Ovid and later I would repeat what he said
Or Ovid would dream
He'd stare at me
Even now he pins philosophical dilemmas on no one but on their interests
I'd dream of birdmen, of watermen, of airmen pursuing women of new shapes
I'd dream of Ovid awake as he opens his mouth and rubs his face on the
          ground
We'd speak of weasels and of stars
We'd speak of Scheherazade
We would shift, giving way to speakers within and to speakers within that
Matter we know would shift
Thought we know would pursue
People fly after their metaphors
But in sleep they seldom realize their dreams
The birds and waters hardly act at all
But stories are transformations
There is *that* preceding the *what* of this
Animal then lull—or lull first, then pull and burial

✻

while people scream at each telephone call
several fat boys in bed play pinball
and their mothers are summoned to pay a fee

the children naturally want to see
and we can't deny them the burlesque show
since we've already promised to let them go

✻

Human curiosity contradicts the human will to believe
But what's the denial of solving
It is a happiness to wonder
Night visions rhyme
And because of their obscurity they seem uncanny
They undertake that more than mathematical spreading of pattern that
        seems to be the root of all beauty
It lets us mock and destroy the utterly complete
With night thoughts like these, are we not logicians?

Is the sleeper leaning to make contact with reality?
Everything is scattered beyond the face
Detached
But persons have their immortality to sacrifice—and why stop?

Bibetgekess

❉

Inside my body are hellish viscera whose flames burn
everything I eat. O fly, enter my mouth
and go to hell. O grape, roll back
on my tongue and descend. I exhale
the smoldering fumes of all I've consumed.

✻

The lamb butts its head against the udder. The human baby nuzzles the nipple, rubs its lips back and forth over it, mother and infant enjoy mutual pleasure. That's how it works: the nipple stiffens, releases milk. There are low, amorphous clouds clinging to the south, neither dissipating nor getting any closer. We hit rain about 40 minutes north of home. The traffic got dim, ghostly, the road at times seemed like a flourish in an hallucination, apt to change in an instant as the result of some unpredictable gesture. But I want to underscore the words that Tolstoy is said to have underlined in his encyclopedia so as to remember what underlies this: *social reality determines consciousness*. Off we go, into the mountains, to escape social reality. At the end of time, the sky will burn like a sheet of blue paper. We have each contributed to what has become our literary history things inherited from our own individual history. Irony and pathos—the two are never far from each other. It's rare now that when I wake the morning seems to greet me by exclaiming "Bingo!" Are we each guilty of a different failure? One of us too skeptical, another too assertive, another too friendly (a form of cowardice). But why make a failure of one's virtues? Perhaps because we imagine they will mar the view, the view in which we figure, the way a nuclear power plant does the coastline or an oil drill the Montana plains. Five robins and some starlings land on the grass just outside the window under stormy skies. I do not say they are "just robins and starlings." The contemporary writer continues to struggle against sentimentalism and didacticism, but, out of sight and hearing, they seem to be thriving. The terrifying beauty of the mountains near the sea weakens travelers. "I don't want to say anything," says a traveler coming upon a view of a violet-hued precipice, stunted cypress trees clinging to its sides. Travelers begin to speak because they want to fall silent and feel compelled to say so. The incommensurable is that which resists or eludes assimilation by way of comparison (e.g., "that is just like Y!"). The incommensurable can't be incorporated into the realm of exchange value, of the commodity, it resists the submergence of everything into that system of equivalence, which nullifies uniqueness and compels us to exchange, for example, this beautifully made table for that tenderly nurtured cow. Promises are always weak, and they weaken the future. Where Bruce Andrews's work *bares the device* (of social oppression) at the lexical and phrasal levels, Barrett Watten's *bares the device* (of something more recalcitrant and thus even more devastating) at the structural/semantic level. Andrews shows how fucked up the language with which groups speak is; Watten shows how tragic and fucked up our very structures of thought are. The sea, for example, is a very dark gray, its far edge clear and hard against the horizon, where light's reflected off the clouds. Rain falls, releasing pleasure incommensurable with our fucked up structures of thought. I perseverate on rain, I perseverate on pleasure. Why did Gertrude Stein determine to eliminate memory from the processes of cognition? Perhaps because she had been unhappy. Bird and animal similes are said to aid remembrance. Think how melancholy the phrase "That was all long ago" is. A young person dies, and a life is lost. Like her, we have lost her life; she has none apart from the one she once had and we now remember, but that is *that* life but not this one. Say you go to a graveyard, a cemetery— do you step on the graves or walk around them? The wind is blowing from the south. If trees are not homes to dryads, then it's perfectly okay to cut them down. I had a dream in which I was required to give a five-minute disquisition in Latin on the term doctor. I didn't think I could do so and then a phrase suddenly came to me: *doctor bonus est.* I was enormously pleased. Then I remembered that by changing the word order I could make a more interesting, more punchy statement: *bonus est doctor, bonus doctor est.* Suffice to say that Adorno's entire project as a philosopher and critical theorist involves a critique of domination; his work is an indictment of the multiple ways in which humans dominate nature, each other, and even their own selves. A typical family saga begins at a wedding. By the end of the day the family is more complex and soon the bride will be pregnant. But her happiness is trimmed with anxiety. As the wind increases, so will the height of the waves, the drama of the spray. True heroines, however (perhaps serendipitously, because we have ended up talking about love, as if *that* were to be the term of ultimate judgment)—true heroines are never petrified. And the marriage is not, in fact, the true beginning. First the sun came up. The night before that it rained, but the storm passed and by dawn the leaves on the trees in the park appeared to be juggling beads of gold light in the breeze. That's descriptive. One should picture each moment as a bundle quivering in the breeze, then disappearing into what Tolstoy termed "labyrinths of linkage." Then the bird flew away. We (all things) exist in an historical/temporal continuum, true enough. But it behooves us not to be subsumed by it. We must each retain (and be granted) our uniqueness, even as we retain our relevance—which is to say our interrelatedness. At the moment, I'm standing on a ledge, and at the bottom of a small but deep pool of clear water I can see the openings of tunnels leading further underground. The sides of the pool are invisible; I'm standing on a shelf of rock overhanging the pool; the ground on which we stand is just a thin crust, and it could collapse at any point. A twisted cypress stands to the left of the outcropping overlooking the sea; it is very old. It leans to one side and is sere on the side facing the prevailing winds. It may never have been finished before its destruction began. If literature has a holy task, it is to resurrect the dead. I watch a black-shouldered kite; it hovers over the field, then plummets, landing hard, feet first, pauses, and then ascends, gripping a dark mouse. Onto the concert stage, mid-sonata, steps a vagrant fiddler who, superfluous and shy, like a child at the fringes of her parents' party, begins to play. What the sea promises, it will provide, which is more than one can say of a *painting* of the sea—one of Turner's, for example. That's what is so miraculous about the painting. It's a rainbow, but with durability. Wind whistles through the rigging. I'm reminded of a desolate abandoned amusement park a friend and I came upon at the edge of an icy field in Sweden. It couldn't have been past 3 in the afternoon, but already it was getting dark. How vacantly the swings hung, swaying slightly. The cyclone fence continually quivered. The vagrant fiddler is a ghost in the *theatrum mundi*, and he is playing something vaguely familiar.

✻

A voice says, The ambered bed flag fills.
A voice says, This is voltage island.
A voice says, The wall past which little girls flick is built of baffling bricks.

✵

Throughout the ages, works of the imagination have been taken as proof of something.

Sunlight sparkles on lukewarm jets wobbling over drinking fountains, while visitors to the park seem preoccupied, busy in the ever-abandoned space.

Here lies a field in otherwise dry sunlight, there hangs a target affixed to a bale of straw resting on a pair of sawhorses. It is in the nature of the straw to rest. In whatever situation straw is used, in whatever configuration it is organized or strewn, no matter how susceptible it is to disturbance, it comes eventually and repeatedly to rest.

The target, its circles concentrated on the surface of a straw-stuffed square, is unassailably isolated, inassimilable, forever separate from the straw within, as well as from the trees behind it, the buttercups on the ground under it, the buzz in the air around it—perhaps of bees or the breeze that comes up toward the end of the day.

The target's concentricities invite and then narrow one's focus.

A visitor who wants to impress the ranger by asking an intelligent question approaches precipitously, with one hand raised.

There are plenty of people who are content merely to pat the ranger's horse, or hold their children back, out of the way.

But things requiring imagination don't just *happen*.

Everywhere there is imagination it is evident in a sort of willfulness.

Suddenly the imagination suggests that I compose a sentence using the words *captivity*, *awe*, *city*, and *goose*, and I imagine the minute scrapings of a condemned prisoner.

Daylight tests the imagination; the imagination, in turn, targets the dark.

If the dark is an obstacle—as fear might be to the over-sensitive or lassitude to a mourner—one has to pass belligerently right through it, registering nothing.

The dark does not invite common sense, though it may require that it be utilized, as machine guns are in times of war.

In a tale told on the threshold of the dark, deeds of heroism are undertaken by a poetry-spouting warrior.

Ring out the kings,
Ringlets should be pretty—
Off with the ringlets of the kings!

O sir bourgeois!
You are just as dirty—
King of the thing of things!

His clear voice echoes off the walls of the prison, just as the inexhaustible relativity that surrounds ordinary things is what locates them. The imagination can find this warrior, though not without some difficulty.

Freedom of the imagination requires practice, experience. "I am giving you a song and I'm taking the gun," sings the warrior. "And so I leave the laughing-room with its echoing walls, where each can show off to an audience of lovelies."

✳

The twenty-third night was very dark.
It was cold.
My eyes were drawn to the window.

I thought I saw a turtledove nesting on a waffle
Then I saw it was a rat doing something awful
But anarchy doesn't bother me now any more than it used to

I thought I saw a woman writing verses on a bottle
Then I saw it was a foot stepping on the throttle
But naturally freedom can be understood in many different ways

I thought I saw a fireman hosing down some straw
Then I saw it was a horse grazing in a draw
But it's always the case that in their struggle to survive, the animate must
        be aided

I thought I saw a rhubard pie sitting on the stove
Then I saw it was the tide receding from a cove
But although I have strong emotions when I watch a movie, jealousy is
        never one of them.

I thought I saw a bicyclist racing down the road
Then I saw it was a note, a message still in code
But sense is always either being raised to or lowered from the sky

I thought I saw a gourmet chef smear himself with cream
Then I saw it was myself just entering a dream
But we all know that the imagination when left to itself will brave
        anything

✳

I am having difficulty staying asleep. I repeatedly catch myself saying, as if in a clichéd rhetoric of self-definition, "I am under foreign skies" and "I want to break this pattern." It's infuriating to speak in clichés, but slippage occurs just at the point where the thought of saying something "better" intersects with the cliché and instead I find that I'm attempting to say in Russian, "Sleep arms us with a terrible freedom." I'm in a public tent or under an enormous awning "open to the wind," I say, but then correct myself and say "open to the neck," when what I really want to say is "billowing." It's a "richly aromatic" market, I say, since I smell dusky smoke from apricot seeds roasting over charcoals. Around me are nomadic traders. I know them to be men "of high ideals" (that's the phrase I want but it comes out as "witnesses to revolution," which I recognize as an attempt to inflate the scene with a "whiff of importance." I point to a fruit that at first seems to be a pear, but it is shinier than a pear, it's more like an apple, red and orange and yellow. I don't know the "fluency" here (meaning currency), I don't know if one 123 dinars is a good price or not, and I'm clumsy at counting out the coins, having to take off my glasses to see the denominations and then dropping some coins in the dust. A little girl with what I can't help but call "a serious demeanor" helps me and I smile at her because I can't speak the language (I don't even know how to say the basic words for "hello," "goodbye," or "thank you"), but in some cultures smiling in public is inappropriate and I'm beginning to feel "unwanted," by which I mean that I'm furious with myself. I give the little girl the doll (that's what the fruit turns out to be) and her mother nods "with silent approval." "I'm glad it's not a *talking* doll," I say, thinking the batteries would die in the desert, but they don't seem to understand.

❊

To catalogue affinities I'd call everyone
Janet with a deaf ear and Misha
and Violetta whose neatness takes up a lot of space and Ed
and Joanne who fears the sun and Mary Ann
and Josh and Franco if he'd just speak up
and great-aunt Maureen with only one hand
and the plumber Phil and Xavier the pimp
and Sam in the fog arriving from the West and Lola cycling round
the world so small it quivers and comes to rest
after it falls from the hands of Nestor the juggler
at the sound of drums.

The rhythms are so thick that hawks
and the voices of Mom and Gram are caught up in them
and when Dad moves his shadow spreads and when he swears his words
sound and are the same as the names of Grampa Umberto
and Zina and Declan and Maggie but Juan is
going and so are Luciana and Ping and the warrior Malkam
under a parasol. I wouldn't slight Emil
though his proximity produces anxiety nor forget Corinne
whose narcissism bears forgetting
as it would if she were a dog.

Condensations occur in any catalogue
and changes: championship: Rose
a gear on which one might only be a cog
and Malachi Rebar, Cyprian Betty, Wang Yi.

❉

There are seven new messages
The gypsy turns her head, closes her eyes
The three judges have each been given a slice of dark cake
It's impossible to predict whether the important part of any message will be
        found in the first half or the second

Go
For the million dollars it would take to buy a house overlooking the sea one
        could take a $3000 seaside vacation 333 times
In one of the trillions of trillions of dreams dreamed last night (February 5)
        an ornithologist revealed that sandhill cranes perch only in pear
        trees but in waking life this fact did not bear out
The men in the field are too sad to flaunt farming

Did you read the article
The horses sink, lift left forefoot and step catlike to the right, and speed
Slowly
Then in quick succession spooky music, chirping crickets, a scream, the
        sound of a gunshot...
It's a soundtrack working its movie
The hurdy-gurdy turns, the messages play back

※

    Now in bed suddenly I remember having rescued a spider from the bathtub this morning. I imagined that I had established rapport with my environment. I observed the spider eerily. I was in harmony with my life and times. Not only will things go on but this going on will repeat.

    After all, I can vow kindness in relation to something I cannot know.

    The spider, when it appears within "a range of alternatives," will be rescued—dished out of the nicked and polished porcelain tub and knocked onto the shrubbery just outside the open window.

    Of course, it will not be the same spider each time but one in a sequence of spiders.

✳

The world is between tips
We say so to know
We go to look over or out to its pivot, to its wobble and drift
Terrible
We are leaving
There's nothing to come to there but transformation and tint
Seductions
So we can't be repeating
What one knows in this state can't be known in another
Time matches nothing

A person circles sleep to pines or tides in entered light
Thousands depend on one
Repeated
And all that's repeated is mediated
Thought
The order is such that it situates
At the farthest extent of a scene are its reachings
Night life is search of its kind
Reach
A gesture not of things but of crevice, preface, prelude
I imagine without standpoint, poised at loss point, at pole
And the horizon doesn't hold there
Its gaping point of contact spreads the latitudes
The pole is interminable, coming and going to arrive
It shares the mobility of an oblivion I want to witness

✳

Once there was a goose who floated midstream from the moment she woke to the moment she slept.

Once there was a girl who knocked a spider into a river and was thus compelled to put a leaf between her teeth and swim far out into the current holding her head above the stream to rescue it.

Once there was a family gathered in a small backyard and once there was a turtle on a log and when the family and the turtle are mentioned one after the other the turtle flops off its log and the members of the family laugh.

Each such episode suggests a moment in an imaginable universe—or, rather, each fills an imaginable and not (by our standards) unreal universe with its own uniqueness, and each uniqueness has staying power.

Once there was a branch that fell into a stream and the new patterns that swirled around it spelled a name that drifted downstream and disappeared around a bend and no one every spoke it nor knew whose it was.

Once there was a detective on a bridge who longed to tell everyone everything he knew and therefore he started running across the bridge as fast as he could.

✻

The scavenging beetle is as big as a thumb
It's dangerous to ride on a brittle beetle bone
Bone, thumb, coat
That's the coat

✳

As the alarm clocks go off we say to ourselves it's time
Or to each other we say it
And, elbows to bed, hands to head
Nude, nightgowned, or pajamaed, we rise, some
To the left, some to the right
As if into a dream
Or out of many
And why?
When we sleep like geese
We're free, when we wake
Like geese
We feed
On wheat
And milk which we find melancholy
And why?
It's viscous and white and thick it shines
Back at us its round and simple placid face
Which we can scarcely irritate
Or imitate
Though we bare our teeth, take it on our tongue, grow gray with age, and
        die like paper turned to ash
Taking flight
As all things must
That are white
As cumulus clouds, flat at the bottom and round
On top they rarely produce
Precipitation evaporating
As the sun sets
Through a broken ring
Smashed by a hammer hitting the hand
Of a woman once
A girl and that girl once
A bride who married a simpleton named Napoleon
Or Ned who led a life
Of scholarship eating candy and drawing circles
Whose value has increased so much that now, at 7:15 on March 28, each
        is worth 71.5 times more than it was around
A quarter

Of a century ago
And why?
Ghosts are made of light and disappear
As the sun shines
Achieving new naiveties—butts bare, butt holes exposed
To alarming shittings
Of embarrassing excrement
Dropping in dreams
And why?
Between the buttocks lie secrets we cannot keep to ourselves
Of experiences
That knock us on the brow, that resonate
And we let them—we can't help it—
See how the film running
Back shows ripples closing
In like initiates to a circle or animals
To a pool
From which they're chased back out by a man with a stick
And why?
Because he has a stick
And he's a man
And those are animals—a gazelle
Is among them, and a camel, a poodle, and more women
Than I can name Hilda, Crystal, or Diane
About whose neck hangs an instrument designed for seeing birds
On the wing or on the branch
Of the family tree on whose green boughs my grandfather
Publicly
Grumpy
And sweet
In the yard
Found some inedible fruits—unripe
When placed in the basket
As a child tucks a doll
Like Samantha (born in 1904) or Nellie (born 1906)
Both of whom come by mail with a book (see americangirl.com)
That adds to the story
Of life
A nineteenth century fiction
That they helped to make history when time too was young
And tomatoes were inedible

✳

Reasoning is the blank sense over a "hot spot"
It's like a gear with petals

Loose history dreams logical desire
     of privilege
     of preface
     of electrical currents
     of punishment
     of a machine that is designed to bring about a fall
     of the rays of the sun or of stars
     of volume
     of reflected light

❇

frst Vhtidyinr — nr erll
I mean …
mpe jrsy smf dp, ryjomh nsf

But there is no way to correct a dream

✻

I saw a juxtaposition
It happened to be between an acrobat and a sense of obligation
Pure poetry
Of course there is a greater difference between an egg and a napping man

✻

But isn't midnight intermittent
Or was that just a whispered nine
A snap of blown light low against the flank of a cow
A likeness of something numberless that only I not knowing the sound
    might know
It may have been howled by a circling dog being chastised — threatened —
    by multiples of itself in pursuit of the consolation of knowing that
    everything is real
It was real
I don't mean midnight — despite horizon, nipple, and fissure
I don't mean
And yet I do — mean, I mean
A cowering animal woven real
    flickers
            please pull over
                Kierkegaard
Kierkegaard says knowledge precedes every act but surely there are acts that
are not preceded by knowledge. Repetitions pass at the door from summer
to winter. Some slowly. Some quickly. Total strangers. Never saw them
before. Can't picture them now. Umbrellas — strange totalities — upheld,
wheeling.

✳

The wife of the merchant George sat plotting. The merchant George stood ironing. Their daughter Little Greta was in the corner playing with a roll of film. Snip, snip, snip. One frame after another fell onto the table. This is pleasant secretarial work, said Little Greta, chewing the end of one of her braids.

Klondike! Klondike! said the parrot.

The merchant George had received the parrot as a gift from a morose lawyer in San Francisco who claimed to be descended from Jack London.

Descended is the operative term, said the wife of merchant George, who was a cynic. She was never envious but often jealous and she was apt to become stricken with grief whenever the merchant George was away from home even slightly longer than expected. Like Penelope, she kept a loom in the bedroom, and she displayed her passions by weaving flamboyant fabrics. She called them displacements and regarded them as proof of her emotional maturity.

George, you are an emotional baby, she said, as she settled Baby Samuel onto her lap and slid his first taste of rice cereal across his lips.

Skeptically, Baby Samuel spat it out.

What, I wonder, has happened to them all. Is it the same thing that has happened to me?

❉

Love rules below and the frogs groan
The frogs groan flat

✻

Everyday I cannot bring myself the wildlife of the wilderness
Nonetheless we are evil enough
Other things come to us—are we not adequately humanized?

We are human attractions
But what has escaped us
What has remained outside?

I could say that phenomenologists have had some wild attitudes, but
          those can't be reversed
Herds no longer cover the landscape
The last bear was driven from these hills in 1949

And now I feel opposed to using slang or italics for mere noisy
descriptive emphasis
I'd rather save them for replications of precise animal sounds—the nasal
          wieyiennnnnnh of the mosquito's song, for example
But is our love of Nature reciprocated?

Apart from those few mosquitoes in the area we seem to be alone
Still, if one were to abolish the real world one would have to abolish logic
The night is always neutral to us—its dark is a field or sheet of a different
          commotion

In a mingling of images an owl appears which seems to be a salmon
It charges through the mountainside with the energy of the totality of
          what it's become
By dawn it's all a blur, the clarity as clear as the purport of a
          mockingbird's yodel

The sunlight sustains the howl and rampaging of clarity
So now it looks as if a heron is visible in the tree
But no—it's only an interference—an upright stubby branch in the crown
          of the tree

But why only that, why privilege the bird—the tree too is interesting in
          this survey of grasses and industrious bugs
The daily survives its compelling collapse in the wild moonlight
It creates its wild collapse in the compelling daylight

✻

For the Timtarians oppressed by the Planch, the claims of the dissident Planch intellectuals are unconvincing. "Where was your magnanimity," asks a dark Timtarian named Gus, "when our poor marched into your cornfields?"

Dissidence, when it has entered historical memory, can only be represented by fragility and mournfulness.

The Planch plutocracy will in the end be brought down by fragility and mournfulness.

❋

When I speak it's clear that I don't reject
the world. Its witnesses
Coincide with this. We all enjoy illumination
and visibility. At the park
A shuddering infant watches the leaves, a child
floating on an inflated dinosaur
Slowly crosses the lake—alert, submissive,
bound. Life takes a real world.
The edge turned toward the wind is sharp, its
opposite dissolves
Into other things—only pretending to be trying
to get out of the way.

✽

the sky gaily nods
                ...eggs

        to yield!

naked
        overjoying indifference

                its honors

                        hairs anywhere

the assassin feathers—
                eight minutes
                after an instant's hesitation

❀

Out of a cavity, here is a case, an oblivion
Its placidity is undisturbed though willing and here is the face recording
    its cast shade
Above is a yellow sky and now the case gapes
Here are the viscera
The curious parts are bisected though the case is without opposites,
    remarkable now and between us, its name irrational
The name comes unimpeded and goes observing out, there an arm, a leg

❈

Climate and alibi.

Application—what a laugh!

Fixation (the first repair), then elegy.

Rattled elegy!

There's no stopping the entire night
        It goes into a scenario so

                you are pale, prolonged
            at irregular elevations
                    —(how

    are we fixed?)
           —looping
        to contain
      (push, bite, sleep
               around)

                  this night

    and melodious but sometimes…

the impression on the bed sends the moving cups

    —the maintenance
of which keeps us—

    off to see what fills them

    comes to a standstill

breathless, motionless, diligent
as persons facing and sleep backing out—

      not over
      forgetfulness
          (forcing
          memory on someone else)
       but across
          nervous linoleum.

✳

Sleep is vast for two in allegiance

✳

Donde est mon cher chou-chou,
The one whom ya vye lyublyu —
Ohn on the road, mojet beet he will call
Ay moi, ya yemu skaju all.

✾

There once was a woman who waited for sleep, but it was away at war
Sleep didn't return
On the pillow there were only her own dark hairs

Each morning the sky was devastated by light
As soon as this was so, she left her bed without sleep

Sleep used to come for only a short space and time, but without illusion
Now there is only illusion
Dreams and heads
This is already endless

The woman, panting, turns in her room, thinking of sleep
Thousands of moths raising dust from their wings flutter and crawl over
        the glossy black surface of the sky leaving pale smudges
Moths gather at a blind dream for settled sleeplessness
The woman remembers heat, the body of sleep, its chest, its breath—but
        sleep is at war, sleep only embraces antagonists

Overlapping is all that lasts; the ghost of everything else occurs in a flash
Off in the distance, sleep roars

✳

Perhaps someone wrong enough is right to be wrong

Perhaps nations ought not to hunt people they care nothing about

Necessity is a state of incapacity but perhaps incapacity is a state of
 necessity

Everything changes but perhaps the whole remains although it seems
 unlikely as well as undesirable

There is nothing but reality

Once there was a man named Task-in-Life and there is no perhaps about
 that

There can't be perhaps about anything that is

But perhaps there is

Perhaps this Task-in-Life was a poor soldier with holes in his boots, a bad
 back, and warped arrows

Every proposition comes to an end but perhaps the end brought about by
 a negation is more of an end than an end brought about by an
 affirmation

Something cannot be more or less of an end so the end announced by yes
 and the end announced by no are equally false ends

Perhaps there was once a horse named Predication but perhaps it was
 called Trepidation or Shadow

Loyalty tolerates a degree of doubt in its vicinity but doubt has a tendency
 to turn a vicinity into a swamp in which a soldier like Task-in-Life
 is apt to get his boots sucked off

If there once was a horse known as High Spot the distinction between
   High Spot and a star would have been clear

High Spot, a mollusk, show tunes, vivacity, and a star

Perhaps affirmation prolongs what it affirms, negation curtails what it
   negates, but the temporal advantage that affirmation has over
   negation is probably insignificant

But perhaps at this point the notion that nothing is insignificant should
   be affirmed

Perhaps noise moves the air, perhaps the air moves noise, and perhaps we
   can have it both ways

Doubt is a source of questions, but questions are also a source of doubt

Perhaps everything ends gradually in a single dilemma but if so the
   dilemma in question is suddenly limitless

Perhaps plants live upside down or perhaps they eat with their feet

✻

Yesterday has arrived and remains
Under suspicion
By the bereft of bereavement, by the adrift of generating distance
That makes description of the shore almost impossible
And of the distance, too, shuddering beyond the tents
Pitched like heads under hats on the sand
And chattering nonsense that we try to interpret
To our continual embarrassment—
We are the idiots here
And the tents and heads and hats and sand
And the water, too, bobbing and sagging
Or nagging, finally, as people do who are sick of themselves
But this could all have taken a different course
And maybe it will
Yet
There are more than the usual number of hummingbirds hovering
Over the morning glory strangling the fence and the sun
Is shining on the pepperwood trees
That offer good shade and cover for fish
In the ripple
Area 80% gravel, 10% rubble, 5% boulder
And 5% silt
And a full 100%
Of dreams occur at such times as these
When one's asleep, a state
For which we have a term, imperfectly
Understood
During which one expresses no discomposure
Except perhaps for a slight twitching of the eyelids, compression of the
        mouth, occasional grinding of the teeth, changes
In the depth and rate of inhalation and exhalation and (rarely)
        comprehensible (though mumbled) speech
Proving that insensibility is not a site of calm
And lies
On one's side, a witness to a shooting in a savings
Bank near a bank
Of steel

Safe
Deposit boxes sealed
And all much the same
To which waking has no key
As we've no master
To cut from
The sky pure and simple
Or what we call sky and hope
Everyone does so too—how else could we communicate to each other
Secrets
So precise, intimate, and detailed
Their secrecy lies
In its constellation and suffusion
That is impossible for words
To hide
And paint
(Cyan, cerulean, viridian, alazarin lake, etc.)
With passing verisimilitude
Which it can't contain—that's realism—
Which is to say
A fleeting realization
When hate, optimism, mourning, and pleasure wake
One from one's dreams
In which are hidden one's most dire clichés—one's eyes, one's brain, one's
        claims
And they don't respond, refuse
To answer
Even to George, Amelia, Claude, Juan, Janice, or Bob
Though Bob turns back indeed
He flips, falls
Down he goes and immediately he's up
Again, arms out—vengeance is hollow

❁

I ride
a postcard

the last cart
                    a certainty
behind a pony

                        the girls in it
                        don't look serious
                    they look like wild dogs
                    from long exposure

Or a child sucking on a python's tail
At nap time with alertness suppressed
For a moment of rapport
An inflation of sense not attached to its human name

✳

Here we begin

Stop!

Study the human mind

She's gone

I see nothing when she moves the mind from within

She must mean the light to be right

That's not an anthropological view

It's not a hand

Then is this a case of fantasy passing act through impasse

Both

Temptation leaps to the corridors, chaos keeps to control

Narration rings, story on story

The mechanisms pulling

The events occur in relay

The concluding is displaced and delayed

And the observer asks only that things continue

The observer governs

Don't stop

❋

      synonymous

... of vegetable

thinginess everywhere — clutter!
      with vegetables!

surroundings

      in a vision

      and that explains ...

but what kind?

      and would another mind have ...

✻

I insist that I didn't say "political club" but "political run." We wanted to address *all* of those little irritations that distract one just at the moment the sunset is the most beautiful.

I believe that there has never been an historical moment more in need of lawns and gardens for the little ones to run around in after fighting both ideologically and practically against CEOs than this. The lives of the little ones are in a state of *transition* but they shouldn't be thrown into a state of *upheaval*.

Transition is fun, after all, though little ones need reassurance during it.

And, of course, one can't accomplish it in a single burst—that would upset the little ones. And, by the way, it's not something that will make you rich.

Probably you yourself have experienced moments in which a disjuncture between your professional persona (dignified, knowledgeable, experienced) and your persona as a granny (crawling around on the floor honking, pretending to be either a goose or a truck) seems suddenly terrifying to the little ones.

Then one day you'll gallop off, crossing a border from which there is no return.

You'll lose your personality—you'll no longer be vain, demanding, deeply insecure, vividly charismatic, and wonderfully intelligent.

✻

The moon was solemnly full.
Jim Trotmeyer assertively declared, Emotions can't be governed by rules.
Millie Corcoran politely requested, Don't overwhelm me.
To this Jim Trotmeyer delightfully responded, But the azures of spring
            truly rush.
Millie Corcoran remarked astutely, Azures rush, yes, but composedly.
Jim Trotmeyer mused pensively, The clouds do indeed puzzle.
Millie Corcoran said sociably, They appear above the crowd.
Oswald Proskaniewicz interrupted furiously, You, Jim Trotmeyer, are not
            the radical you say you are.

✳

Sleep came
          after all—L

    he heard it

         too. I

        naturally thought

... my eyes

            being ...

on a collision course ...

          with impatience
          I'm hurrying
    "out of it," not sure where to go, what to do. The area at the top
of one tower framed by the crenellated walls can be used as an outdoor
bathtub and this is very convenient. "There's no *way,*" I say, periodically,
looking at my watch. I'm barefoot; my toenails are painted. My father isn't
irritated, although I'd thought he would be—he says he'll go get my shoes,
since I don't know where the car is. There isn't that much time left before
we go to Europe. I feel increasingly hurried. Living is getting gendered
frantically, at increasing velocity and tilt. I think Dad said Europa—or
could it have been Roma?

✻

we will
see out coins

✳

Some people insist on exercising the sincerity of their intentions
No sunglasses
I cannot produce any more posterity than my grandparents could and
       they will not begin to understand
In the course of a beautiful allegory a coursing god kills a child
Children return but only if their deaths are individually acknowledged
Deaths occur in a milieu without laws or so we think, finding them
       scattered unequally throughout the world
We have never yet remained all the way through the sequence of
       vignettes that's said to be their original
One death alone is enough to turn one's brain—we twist our imagination
       to the maximum
We are forced to cry stop but like a horse with a cart the imagination
       trots on

✼

The picture appears suddenly in its entirety
It begins nowhere, and I'm faced with it
I'm against the wall opposite it facing an audience and replying to the many
       objections that the audience is lodging against existentialism
The picture raises no such objections, being ridiculous in its own right
It is there by virtue of a mere fluke with silent placidity
The picture is of a cow then?

I have to turn away

A cow?
Then?
There's a cow on a board?
Board, certainly, but no cow, and we term that a picture?

That it's of a cow rather than a battle is not a disappointment

Life needs PR, an advertising campaign, promotion, encouraging slogans:
       Live it, bovines!

I neglect to do battle willingly out of cowardice

I'm avaricious, I want the picture

I would settle for a picture of the picture

✳

My mother keeps her folded bicycle in a clear plastic package in her purse
I'm wearing a black dress I bought from a judge and already the hem is
       coming undone
I swoop past two women who are throwing lemons at a man

We are on a family outing to a pair of frozen lakes
There's to be an art exhibition, a traveling blockbuster, the ad for it shows a
       child running, she shouts, "I Want to See Ra!"
A boy skating nearby suddenly falls and slides a long way across the lake,
       papers fly out of his pocket, and a security guard who helps me
       pick the boy up asks if I have the boy's birth certificate with me

I'm not supposed to be drumming — this is a defiant gesture — but I'm very
       good at it
Loud rhythms can be a brilliant counter to the current xenophobic
       atmosphere in the United States
Someone points out that the new snow has to be pushed around and it will
       take skiers to do it

I'm skating well and swoop around a curve, outer blade gripping the ice
I'm carrying a package I am supposed to give to someone named Winifred
       but I'll never see her again
Awake I find myself re-experiencing the extreme happiness very like grief
       of a dream in which I hike upward through an alpine landscape
       away from my children who are, however, there to welcome me
       when I reach the mountaintop

I pass some kids and shout, "I'm really getting the hang of it," as I follow the
       track onto the bigger lake
I begin with a quiet, subtle rhythm and then bang, I bring up the tempo and
       the music takes off
As we run forward shouting, the police fling their hockey sticks over our
       heads into the snow and the festivities begin

We have won

114

✺

My stomach is important.

If I tell you that I am nagged by worry at night and suffer from stomach pains as a result, it is something you should remember because later people may ask you about me.

Because I'm a boa constrictor.

❈

There are birds in the tree singing as precision
Remain confused I tell myself they say

✻

I formulate statements

    in the dark I shape

the phrase is

       this is

          and the example
       takes shape

A goose at a lectern
    John Coltrane blowing
    bubbles Jacques Derrida
       waltzing are examples

but they are all far more
    than exemplary that's fine

           if one wants more than that there are
geese in the lake I rowed
    with a friend for picturing

           a point worth taking

the waltz is

    a dialectical dance

    in it one keeps
        moving like a point well taken

    one might take anywhere dancing but doesn't

❋

I've come to the right place
          on the right road
                    in the right frame of mind
    or
I've come to the wrong place
          on the wrong road
                    in the wrong frame of mind
    or
I've come to the right place
          on the wrong road
                    in the right frame of mind
    or
I've come to the wrong place ...

You can see where this is going—

I've come to the wrong or right place
          on the wrong or right road
                    in the wrong or right frame of mind

But—no problem!
Here I am!
I've lived long enough that I'm now no more than a self-taught
    shred

Perhaps things are written in the stars but I don't think so and
even if they are I wouldn't know what they said

✻

Once a poignant catalyst was lodged in the Y of a tree
No, not a poignant catalyst — the poignancy of the catalyst, like the catalyzing of the poignancy, came later
A bee landed on a fallen peach
A beloved man struck a table with the flat of his hand
A sailor reached terra incognita without water and found it overrun by sheep
Why?

Causes pursue all wobbly deeds

❀

Just after 5 pm at Blockbuster's there's a line of people waiting to rent movies. I notice that the women, myself included, are all exhibiting sarcasm in relationship to the place—taking a defensive stance and talking tough. We women are in league.

We know what we're in for and we're taking it on our own terms.

My children are grown, but I'm between two mothers (with whom I feel kinship) accompanied by children and the children are pushing at the situation. One little girl around 10 years old asks her mother if she can have her own Blockbuster card (she's just read the blue bulletin board offering a "kid fingerprint card") and her mother says she can, just as soon as she gets a job and can pay for it. The woman in line behind me tells her two children, "This is inside, and where the car is is outside. You can make all the noise you want outside, and inside you be quiet."

I ask the 10 year old what movies she likes.

"Do you want titles or genres?" she asks.

She has a lot of coins wrapped in a red and green handkerchief and a couple of them fall out. A little boy picks them up for her. He asks, "Are you here alone?" and her mother turns around quickly. "Oh," he says, "that's your mama."

We women at Blockbuster's remain suspicious. We're indulging other people's behavior—or we're indulging our own but we're making sure that no one thinks we're fooled.

The men in the place seem to be at ease, relaxed, unguarded and it's not only because the videos for rent at Blockbuster's are predominantly for male tastes.

At Blockbuster's men and women exhibit markedly different attitudes and the issue seems to be control. When I am there I participate in displacements in the context of control. The women in Blockbuster's seem to be asserting control—although the apparent target of their authority is often their children; meanwhile the men seem to want to "go for it," even when they are with children. There's a kind of abandon to men's selection of tapes—they are abandoning criteria, whereas the women keep their criteria to themselves. What they select or reject is nobody's business.

Their criteria have nothing to do with morality. They have something, however, to do with justification—with the difficulty of justifying what they desire.

"I'd rather sleep than watch this," says the woman behind me.

✻

I wake

      for a moment

      As Nestor to his beloved Lethe—

      Lethe, Lethe…

         All the rest I forget

❄

As innocent as rubble is the workshop of oblivion.

At its sunlit bench the stubborn singer holds her breath.

Every stone you lift you owe to destruction.

✻

Once there was an old man who was buried in a bottle under an apple tree. Every summer his daughter came to pick apples off the tree and when her basket was full she would stamp her foot and shout, "Get out!"

The sun shone, the sky was clear. "Perhaps tomorrow there will be a few clouds," said the irritable painter at the edge of the orchard; "if not I will go to a museum to spit at the idiots one can always find there!"

The orchard stood across the road from a sweet-smelling, shadow-filled forest. Motes of light drifted between the trees and a clear creek splashed over sparkling stones and flowed into occasional ponds. The sounds of the water excited the handsome little grandson of the woman who had come there to fish.
"You'll make the fish nervous," she said to him, "You'll catch the fish if you wiggle as they do," the boy replied.

During the night, dew refreshed the orchard. Drops of water slid over the apples and fell to the ground covering the bottle with the old man inside.

"Oh, how long it takes," he said. "But when it's done, it is going to be delightful."

✻

One evening
        at the door

                  so the philosopher opened
            the thinnest man has come over

I thought as much!

        my freedom

                my neck
it's genuine

        do I owe you anything?

    is tenacious

the street outside strewn with smashed apples

        in the hallway

            my name again! he cried

✻

Our would-be sensitivities are social
They are the result of careful observation
Empathy
Say you see someone naked
Check out the webs
Ripple, finger, and jab the ribs
Jiggle the ribs
You laugh?
How did we get to juggling pigs?

❋

I'm almost ready—here—
things come—okay
each thing must reveal itself in order
to begin and then distinguish itself
by being obdurate and endear itself
without omission so as to proliferate
without summary and secure
itself—I'm almost ready—so
as to continue and remain—

✻

A magnificent rodent with a potato in its mouth has scurried over my bed. Its tail brushed my cheek—I think this is what woke me. Now, alert to its presence, I am aware of another one, too.

Two magnificent rodents.

They are incandescent, like flashes of experience. They are creators of reality. I can't judge their size—they are smaller than pigs, greater than bugs.

Further contact between us is impossible. That's one thing of which I'm certain. Contact produces uncertainty.

But one should be aware that some people are delusional without being unhappy.

✽

Isn't sleep fitted to this world?
Aren't dreams a form of internal criticism?
Doesn't each dream catch a previous day of the world in an act of criticism?
Isn't this itself dreamed / criticized by an expert?

✤

Some people are ticklish and it's symptomatic of their sensitivity
They are quick, like storytellers, to express experience
There's evidence that they dream and every day the evidence is accumulating
They need its services
They cannot concoct without laughing at the strength of sleep
Still, the stretch of sensitivity is hard to measure

The senses, inventive, permit us to sleep
They get us into a situation
Among senseless objects, there is still some reality

But senses have objects—everything provides evidence of this
The objects make themselves available and laugh
Suddenly you're one of them

Morbid curiosity makes you watch, though warned
Being what's watching you're watched
As careful as it is to be eclectic you cannot choose
Dreaming of encyclopedias and thumbing backwards—is this what it is to
        have memories?

✤

Shame is gawking. It is petulant
but fervent. What is the fit
to shame, its match, the, so to speak, crime?
Who is forged to violence
and who to fault? Are we lifting frost in supplication
in lieu of lifting voices? Perhaps in the latitudes
of a life we cannot tolerate
a cold infinity prevails. Nothing there
is transient; no one and nothing can return.

✻

She hears a shout, maybe a curse
She closes the window, she feels for the floor

She puts her ear to the window, she puts icing on the cake
She's content to be where she just happens to be found

She sees pigeons in flight, pigeons overcast

And I read about it later: this woman had character!
She preserved desire and eliminated repentance

✻

As for me, I want to be Banambitan
and leave kind ships vitalities by art.
I am untouchable.

✻

Shingles are dazzles on balsa houses.

✳

My personal experiences will take me
only as far as my person goes
who is always slipping
off in the dark
perhaps to serve as a pilot
or setting off as a voyager
whom night has not shut out
from the open cockpit of an obsidian plane
with wings of thick paper covered in scribble
folded in the dark
from which I dangle with skill over a landscape to go to
between days not mistakenly.

❋

to become nonexistent

what is eternity
but that
which is no further followed

✳

Old women don't swing in unison,
too, among others, their deaths
—what loves! sitting quite—
always quite—in a toybox
                    they strike
for the dance against its walls
—brightness of earth, a patter
over the boards of glass accident—pace
slow in the large room
                    there

✹

innumerable and infinite little ants —
      tawny, sharp-snouted,
                       dog-toothed, ubiquitous,
            goose-necked, long-winded
   and eared
      —like rats

✻

Visibility has made waking good
Now an animal pleasure prevails
It measures the kind of time and space one thinks one has a right to
It complicates the ten thousand things that come from the ego
Shadows spread across the empty wall, signs of a false absence
Our disoriented perception goes where it goes
It sees a grove of trees that we associate with shows of kindness, signs of
    real river banks
But doesn't visibility block our view?
And who did I think I'd signal and supplicate
For roads into the other world I can't depend on mirrors
Waking implicates me in all that's here

✺

I pamper myself by completing mundane tasks
I pose before "the judge" or "the editor" but dogs leap out and I am
      immediately apologetic and willing to pay even more than the
      thing is worth
I leave a big tip which simply flaunts my empathy
Sentimental people wage war against numerous evils and they count them
The count might come out 9 dead, 30 injured, and 100 sick, or there might
      be no one dead, but endless injustice
My empathies are banal, they are derivative and inconsequential
I want to succumb to the intoxicating bang! bang! bang! of an action it is
      unwise to take
Its incongruity might be added to my account, it might serve as an
      accomplishment
But when I pose as "the author" I'm sure to exaggerate

✳

The dark is high when the clouds have blown so the darkness can descend
There's darkness then accomplishing
Dark descends without abstention
It's really then

✳

Once there was a yellow fortress which stood on an island between the shores of a cold gray river running through an ancient city. In fact, it is there still. The walls of the fortress run straight down to the water and in the fortress are many empty rooms.

At the moment the river is swollen and turbulent; war has caused heavy rains, and many citizens are mournfully swimming. Among them is a woman in a red blouse — she is trying to hold a canary in a bird cage at the end of a long stick above the flood. Another, younger woman in a blue cap is holding onto an inner tube with one hand and attempting with the other to paddle with a pot.

The river is cold and public.

Soldiers manning the fortress walls have been equipped with black rubber bows that are easy to draw, but their wilted floppy arrows droop harmlessly from the bows.

The authorities are sacrificing everyone.

In such a situation sleep is impossible.

Many women as the war began wanted to protest and, gathering together, they did, pointing out the arbitrariness of battle, the inadequacy of the battle plans, the laughable positioning of the weapons, the pathetic brevity of the outcomes of all events.

While demanding their right to eat, to peace, to sex, to dress, to dream, to sleep, they were forced to applaud as the warships retook the sea.

A dream may be a city without citizens, but it has a river to maintain.

In the end, the soldiers entered the beds of the women and turned over and over—or the women did, or the women turned the men.

No one could interrupt this alone.

And yet it still wasn't sleep.

✿

Eventually we close, as if glorious—all possible references
made and pointless as the very slightly more difficult weather
(which is not today's, we say, after some perhaps awkward
usage that makes us way too visible in what is after all mere
milieu). We pull the thread, if there ever was one,
that might have guided us through the murkiest of all either/or
situations. The dust swirls whenever we say something as we
know we must suddenly and lacking subject too though we're
carrying forward one that came on earlier in a wave of ideas.
That's what we call speech sometimes during brief sunny sleep
on days as cold as sand when every vivid specificity and unease
returns, 'pure' but without the same bright clarity
and clowning and juggling that make up their own rules
when restoring sight too completely, producing evidence
that bears only a slight relation to this
real day, which first appeared yesterday, when we were
in every way frustrated that a day, with its enormous physical
and psychological influence, couldn't reorder visible things
or reverse the irrevocable, but that too is clogged with cold sand.

✳

Now it's dark and there's someone in it.

❄

The boy in the warehouse has changed his name from Frank to Ungoverned Flame He has numbed his lips to anything less, he weeps for arrows though he draws up dogs.

The boy in the warehouse never goes out, in his lemon tantrums he calls for everything.

There are fixed limits to his safety, and the dogs, gentle diesel communists, guard the stairwells.

Dogs: Please amplify and clarify and do not simplify or fortify because that's our job: we're going out there, mushrooms and spinach, the fire's raging, the child's been murdered, please eat some pudding, Joan lives on Jones Street, her house is yellow.

House: I stand at the center of a demonstration on behalf of urban farmers.

Dogs: To keep away ants set the four legs of your bed in water and don't let the blankets touch the floor.

House: The elderly can't afford to be frivolous.

Communists: The people are not comfortable.

Ungoverned Flame tunes his siren. There is nothing further, then, to discuss, compromise is impossible, the warehouse fills with noise.

Communists: All knowledge must be continually exacerbated, lest one feel nothing in response to the word "house."

House: A truck drives by and then goes up a waterfall. Barges follow upstream carrying animals, one animal per barge, all headed for the slaughterhouse.

Me: My mother and I have just rescued a horse which is now feeling very relaxed although it has a bandage around its head. We pet it and its swift thick previously belligerent white mane sways gently in the breeze.

Horse: There may be some slight informal significance to this gesture, some social kindness intended.

House: People should be encouraged to get up from their wooden chairs and talk to each other, so if you are carrying a beverage tray hold it high.

The boy in the warehouse, Ungoverned Flame, makes a sketch of the house in his journal of secret postures.

❀

I have this to say but I do not know when to
There was a great forest that I went to
I may never return there but I want to
I have just one memory of it and I want two

※

Lyn? Lyn? Come here! Is that you? Lyn?

✳

When we want something we have to reckon
With probabilities watching
For repetitions observing
Rocks causing ripples
In the stream of consciousness
Occurring over sand
And submerged things
In the shallows
Where our best hope of finding what we want lies
To tell the truth
Where we care the least—
Hear world, see
Whorl
While saying who
We are—hardly worth mentioning—say
Chicken-Licken seizes power
If not legally then at least to the degree that her fear obliges her friends…
Passerby: Are they pleased by it?
Farmer: Are they doing all their tasks as required?
Turkey-Lurkey: Run Goosey-Loosey—or Lucy
Froggy-Boggy: Are you sad? Don't be sad. Why are you sad?
Toady-Roady: Jump, Snakey-Shakey
Sluggy-Wuggy keeps her cool between the long leaves of the irises
         growing along the edge of the path
Gecko-Flecko with ready tongue basks in warm gray sand listening for
         bugs, suddenly
As an incoming missile explodes, the gray horse
Shadow, the brown horse
Duke, the black horse
Prince, and the sorrel horse Rondo in terror
Stampede blindly
Run, Bunny-Money, shouts Piggy-Jiggy
Run, Sheepy-Sleepy, weeps Goaty-Throaty
Because sorrow and anger are very much the same
As animals
When we are misled
At a frantic pace
Into a completely impossible, implausible situation

✳

I am not fatalistic
I recognize addition and in addition I recognize things as different from
      one moment to the next in no fixed sequence as a peanut from a
      plummet of the sun
I cannot help but go out

❄

Sometimes dogs eat melon rinds and apple leaves but though I know this there has never until now in the dark been an occasion on which I could "happen" to say so unless I were willing to interject the information into conversation as a non sequitur and I'm not since that would contribute nothing to the general good. Talk among us, perhaps at L's or K's or perhaps here at home, no matter the degree of animation, no matter the force of our agreements or disagreements, is all intended for the general good. There was talk the other night about forests. B so strongly disagreed with A's opinion that the adaptation of birds to blighted environments can be regarded as progress that I thought she was going to cry. Then M interjected that his friend T considered vinyl superior to CDs, and R cracked, "Hurray for crackle." That was an unpleasant moment, R's tricks can sometimes be harmful, though I am never able to tell in retrospect whether R has been malicious or clumsy and I certainly never see things coming. Things in my particular experience don't make ordinary approaches.

❀

This comes after a feeling of vigorous apathy, the joy of being
immobilized, bound, an object
of striking surprise, an object of fact even
a creature observing illusions in the surf
and a group of persons eating peaches
in its reflections, torpid bodies
with active upcast minds, their random thoughts
vindicated by the inevitable meanings adhering
even to nonsense. Then comes the sad loosening
of the bonds, the attachments
having seemed so logical slip.

✳

Is it unacceptable and does it hurt?
Does it make you sleep?
It is hardly dark and already the body is haunted
Divided by the sun it can hardly rise

The body is dead but its skin is hypersensitive
It contains person already— with permission or not
Details emerge forever
Science

Science, somnabulence, and narcolepsy
Walking on all fours and wondering what one *can't* do
Wanting to part, fully relaxed, with *nothing*
If pain, then time
If time, then vision
Then story, then moral
But someone else maintains the moral

Moral: Isn't it true that no act can have a name which can be said to represent it, since a name, to be of any use at all, must remain constant, while every action is both practically and perceptually inconstant, changing from one moment to the next?

✻

Below the hill are muscled roofs
and red tins in which nesting birds pinch

but let me tell you something —
nobody's putting conclusions around *my* life

✻

    A woman leans over to paint blue curves between her legs. She will leave them there for a week to test the erotic potential of a particular tattoo she is considering, a freeform tattoo of intersecting lines enclosing spaces that can be colored in differently every day. She imagines the ritual of choosing the colors and applying them.

    Isn't it always the task of history to show us something of what has been previously concealed in a hidden space?

❀

The height of the grass along the path through the field increases at every
    telling
How much can it sustain?
One can surprise it, get on top of it, pin down the hands, blow hard into
    its neck, obeying unconditionally
And in the relaxing aftermath of the violence requiring laughter, the
    chaos of logic subsides
There's also a violence requiring satisfaction
Its skirmishes evade skepticism, originality, and pity

✻

with fish fault thought the what
          be out mind free
spoon halt cups
          bang in space pink

                    and lack pink

✳

I watch—I don't have to be careful—the spy stays behind my eye
I look into the shoes
I place them under the window
They have to point somewhere—why not toward the sea?
The room is placid, the shaft of sunlight between window and wall is clear
Is the dog panting?
Its tongue is wagging at both sides, its tail is between its legs
Have the birds reversed?
Are the birds revived and in the air?
I jam the roses into the sand
Freud would understand this immediately: *Soon the many human waking*
    naughty souls will walk out of isolation.

At first the man in the chair—isn't he hideous?
The chair is a still bulk—plagued by penguins—they are shuffling forward
    into my ear
Along comes a peripheral figure—trying to evade the spy—the car in
    silhouette — a paralyzing shimmer
Rain is falling—just an inch and a half of milk
It's true what the guy says says the guy whom they say is not to be trusted
I get into an angle of shadow

The measures of the night require no space
You think that hadn't yet been revealed to me in those days?
Black grooves, the bare floor
Back up—you too want to communicate?

✻

suppose you are
guiding a blind man's hand
not from love

but from love's parts
it passes unsuspecting
and does the unknown cupping

withholding
releasing
indications

and clues it leaves
behind evidence
of two physical truths

✳

Life must learn history quickly
Reproached and asked
How could we have loved, talked, written, lived
Without the lips that will quickly turn
Gray through which we mumble that
I argue that
I loved quickly and I write that
I wrote almost daily just
As the waves ring against the sand
Like quickly sinking sacks
All identical and each alone
At sea
Never coming in
The same, with one wheel warped and another
Deflated or bigger than its brother
Or sister aboard braids
Flying, locks flopping over
The waggish wheels as they roll quickly
Off the curb that stops nothing
But the stallion blue
And gray which is the spirit of the system
Which is still necessary but must quickly make the best connection possible
Between getting up and frying an egg
As if work were all about keeping extraordinary bodies busy
And revolution no more than a practical joke
Whose cruelty is meant
To humiliate us in our dreams and wake
Us in a sweat because it's true we sweat in revolution
As revolutionaries though we're revolted
By ourselves, each
Other, bother to brother
Signal to sister ("Bring meat!")
But a person is not a sausage as some would have it
Endowed with reason but rather a passion
Though it can still be bitten, even thieves have teeth
Which once extracted can be thrown to the wind
At hand to head around mind so we can see

That there's no truth
To the myth that removal of the upper teeth affects one's view
Of Malta, area 122 sq mi, population (as estimated in August 2005) 398
534; life
Expectancy 78.9
On whose shores Hannibal was born and Paul
Shipwrecked and Napoleon reigned and NATO berths
Its ships in aching notches left or made
Which cannot be relieved by placing aspirin in the mouth
Of Sid, the young marine

✻

Let's think of happy people going to sleep
like Pythagoras to music. When they wake
they become persons and require clothes
and that's what we term wakefulness.

✻

It's dark and the clouds have blown
And so
To meet their views we take a night
Forbid the approach of any hostile footsteps
Pass the night

It is during these hours of deep solitude that more than one head turns
The head comes at murky thick and autumn august calm awake
We head
They head
One after another wet to the left and steady
They've one slow imitative name, the clammy reality "human" and the
        boisterous concept "woman"
Tonight is no better than a spiritual intermediary between a grimace to
        influence the milieu and a gathering of opaque, symbolic
        window panes

❁

History has compass, time speeds past, memory gets lost
For a moment in 1950
Naming something
Not very nice and in 1959
Some kind of madness culminates
In family life and some kind of name
Neither astral nor Arctic but isolated nonetheless
Where we know there are shores way out
At sea over which waves hiss
Onto the sand, hot and still, of a blazing island
Or the black rock
Of a cold one moaning with ice
Which superficially seen is thin and just
H_2
And O
As we skate toward each other
Closing in
On the most complex of facts
And shout O
It is now and the alphabet makes many odd sounds
Lost to history
As the little morning teetering on its spine climbs out of bed
And puts its right foot down on the floor, wincing
And the left, the stronger, follows
Loyally taking the weight together
They carry the morning out with its pen-sized news
Into the light to deliver by bike with luminous spokes
Something full though less
Than the full compass, needles spinning
Until the wheel comes full circle
Or hits the curb just short of that
And crashes just as the headlines hit
The city of particulars that will ever (but not never) be the case
Of necessity that overhangs like pleasure planes from clumsy boats
Rented and released
Like nouns (war, official, patriot, pacifist, piglet, death) into sentences
Very emphatically more obviously artificial

To a very touchy man named Max or Milt or Mike or Matt
Than stained glass windows or wrought iron balustrades or pink
        shoelaces holding black skates
On the feet of a boy on ice now pushing
Off right
Foot slipping left coming
Round, sped by desire
Rising like a hillside
To decipher early
And late off
And on

❈

On the one hundredth night I dream of seven subtitles all in a row. The first is *the long interruption and modernity,* and then comes *the loop of linearity along continental divides,* followed by *the teacher's desk and the social event, the journey from noodles to pasta, mimicry and sibling ties, the temporality of memory and paradox,* and *mystification and hilarity as the commodity form in cartoons.*

❋

here in a sudden of this to Caesar the causer come claims

now gone's the short order diplomat worn green by a janitor subject

discord when it's true has the conspiracy pinned

that is the game part that hurts to the rule in reaction

into the list den it is street the dragging consistency dots

the pocket is but ear to dreams requiring optimistic green

the clouded what to fogbound which walks the ground of even all Dakar

the echo janitor's diplomat straddles three abandoned chairs

✳

I'm clutching conspicuous deletions like a martial artist flipping deceptions.
To keep the plants at least in the distant impression I'm now mugging
privacy at the pedestrians below who might otherwise interrupt
the story. They pass down the exercise corridors between their tightrope
    neighbors.
We live between twelve empty futures and seventeen full ones at least.
I don't welcome the bag mallet's prying. There's a warm silver solstice
and the morning is traditional. The bed dips under the crystal pillow
beside the curving hot knob and comes up
with a remarkable interpretation: the cultural deception
is a scotch tape dispenser sealed in a chocolate egg. Exploding
vehicles in a single light are lost among the foraging bears. Aisles
crusted over with applauding Cheerios carry us
against the zoo, mists writing fairy tales for the Brothers Grimm. We slap
the gooey playmates of the normal aunts, do you remember them?—
overly familiar and with secret offspring. How hungry for distracting libraries
they were, but they remained steady and unpainted, keeping their nervous tics
tucked into a rhythmic monotony of memories destroyed by growing up
something other than Italian. Suddenly habits were dancing
there in them though they didn't dare admit it. The sense
of lost isolation was conveyed to me via the odious entryway
on opposite sides of the lies they told, a part of the neighborhood
in which people waited for a long time sniffing. I remember
the hallways and two photographs seen constantly
and then put in flames. Against the first elegant step
of an otherwise murky climb lay a slow instant pond
and on a million mornings its ripples began to squeak.
Some people are baited, some choose to forget. They are all personified
by a pushy sweet pig of a child whose monument
would be a purely classical protest.

✳

A stream of particulars, a stream of abstractions, and wicked geese
The wicked geese hoot, their feet caught in the ice
A fisherman blows his nose into his palm
A sugar beet floats in a dented pot
For the third time in a month we've called for the fireman—he arrives with
       a yellow flashlight
Surreptitiously I lean against the fireman, then step aside
I will think about this later, afterwards
The thought will be long, it will wind through ten events
An event is something that has some social or ethical quality, forms a
       narrative of compelling interest, and exhibits awakening subtleties
A philharmonic group of girls spins around a pole—this is probably a show
       of nerves
A line of ants crawls along the crumbling edge of newly spread black
       macadam in the playground—that's the whole picture

✳

There in your hand is an emerald hoe. You have gone to the basement, you have come to the window, you have forgotten our names. Everyone but you is seasick, and you aren't because you don't lock your knees as you stand on the deck, you ride the waves, you flow.

There in your hand is a mixing stick, and you live in the land of our mothers and incarnations, and you see things turning: flowers into fate, pebbles into water, ripe berries into people who begin immediately to hunt and copulate and prepare food and quarrel.

There in your hand is a viola bow. You are more than seventy years old now, or maybe half of that, or perhaps a thousand. You are a stranger now, or someone who is yet to appear but of whom we have a premonition, and the children know your name.

There in your hand is a mirror reflecting a cloud. You are moving slowly and also quickly, you live in a barn with legs. You refuse to be bossed around and you spill the ink, word goes out to pigeons or maybe they are penguins who are carrying the message.

There in your hand is a message we can't read. You are as quiet and complete as an egg and when it breaks there in your hand is a tile and on it are our names.

✻

Accident and necessity renew their fatal pact
across rocky islands. Come embark
by a process of elimination and run the red machine
between an angry crow and the witty hen
of art's deceitfulness: *the breeze!*
But it could just as easily have been *the bees!* about the world
before ideas flooded in as correctives
to facts held by the fading vegetation
that took silence into itself: autumn
is obsessively memorizing
and as a live toad is to a wet stone so is a library
to momentary obliviousness that it's a painting. Here we are
where blown from consciousness leaves fall
like images from a dream that cannot be revised and never fails.
It will snow little onions, it will rain roasted lamb
and bottles of wine will age on the vine
and wild horses will graze on the banks of garrulous tongues.
A cowboy on a palomino playing a harmonica
one mile at a time, one day much like another, will recapitulate
our work and character in the home key of A
but as A minor, crossing a terrain, an aesthetic convolution,
having failed to master love with the inevitable note
of hopelessness, and sky and river alike will be milk white.

✳

The curtain is flapping—it slaps against the shaking
pane of the open window. The cruel dialogue continues.
We are subject to the rule of metamorphosis. Somewhere there's a
        Douglas fir
that is a fisherman thinking he's tending his nets, a gecko
that is a carpenter with a pigeon soul. Symbols work
on the soul, true signs of the false or false signs
of the true. What a negation! They are rose-stags! Goat-dahlias!
They are butter and several camels. As duty is to beauty
the weed through dew is to thinking: resolute!

✻

there—so it is—there—just that—in time I've loved
—there—no other but one, an other—no other—there—
better by day by night that too carrying the body, the flamboyance—brain—
there—a falling equestrian dressed in silk and sailing since—this

there when declared near—just that—in a moment
dear—there—no further but an extra—nothing new—rare—
recovered once by dark that hauls—again—there—air, ropes, cups
there a dwindling likeness sent and bared, seafaring since—this

at the merest hint taken racing ahead to a figure aboard—an annoying foible—
there—as if to distribute pink or red equally black—to the rescue
at a rock's pace—there—for a figure moving lips—the wrong way?
weight tipping, impending, the whole meditation—waiting—there

✻

Let's speak of the unconscious and do so consciously
We've all got our nocturnal strictures, our fears
Wheels of green like radiant gravestones lean on my field of vision
Those fears want to be intelligible
Those wheels are seeking names
They imagine things
There are sheets of water no deeper than a shadow, beetles in a jug of
     milk, a clotted spider web, a mountain approaching by boat

Everything I think is wheeled by my thinking it
I watch the wobbling horizon from my unpremeditated circle
Words are a way to keep and to keep rolling
The purple night, the building clouds, the point of time
How should I interrupt "the building clouds"
Dreams surround intelligibility
The will digresses, it maintains its stupendous solitude, its cumulative
     inaction

❉

The dog joined in and tore off the whole of the man's face while the man, his arms clasping it, broke every bone in the dog's body, and there the pair of them lay, near death, each having seized what seemed to be its only chance.

✻

I've reported nearly all that I've learned as long as I was reporting it
Once it reached a ditch
Another time light through small holes ran clear through it
I thought I had a toothache!
Now people work harder than ever and the rents go up
People listen to music powerful enough to shatter stone but it falls silent
People—ah! to have students! to pass on all that I've learned!
But they'd need to invent, add color, replace the lights

✳

we should stop here
and defer still

      ... differ stiff
      ... differentiate stiffly
      ... defecate ... stay

✳

Just as the events of the week absorb suspicion
into the present contents of the alphabet A
to Z, which cannot be any more autobiographical than Luther Burbank's
        new fruits
but must be taken literally as a fiction even
as each is taken figuratively as a fool's face on a body
of abstract notions, so a football player's yard
gaining dash when described as flitting matches
the football player's body to a butterfly theme at a point of
disembodiment
too sardonic and plaintive than is wise
but not placid amid the continuing insecurities of girls
who are still holding back the extravagant equestrian, strong, cheerful,
        and conveying S
to S, transgendered, f-to-m, a sort of Hegel
if he were only alive to hear this
and could manage not only to love us but to show it
with only a frisson of the worry staring us in the face starting at age 5
which is still a little early but who could know
if we managed the transition? Boy couldn't exactly say without Girl
but we never set out to be stupid or lazy and we aren't lazy or stupid yet.

❇

constant change figures
the time we sense
passing on its effect
surpassing things we've known before
since memory
of many things is called
experience
but what of what
we call nature's picture
of the many things we call
since memory
we call nature's picture
surpassing things we've known before
constant change figures
experience
passing on its effect
but what of what
constant change figures
since memory
of many things is called
the time we sense
called nature's picture
but what of what
in the time we sense
surpassing things we've known before
passing on its effect
is experience

✳

The measures of the night require no space, the …
The registers …
The most sundry …
The spectators who've …
The …
The repeaters …

       vague leaders …
       weeds …

The …

       left, the leaves …

✾

A dream, still clinging like light to the dark, rounding
The gap left by things which have already happened
Leaving nothing in their place, may have nothing to do
But that. Dreams are like ghosts achieving ghosts' perennial goal
Of revoking the sensation of repose. It's terrible
To think we write these things for them, to tell them
Of our life—that is, our whole life. Along comes a dream
Of a machine Why? What is being sold there? How is the product
        emitted?
It must have been sparked by a noise, the way the very word "spark"
Emits a brief picture. Is it original? Inevitable?
We seem to sleep so as to draw the picture
Of events that have already happened so we can picture
Them. A dream for example of a procession to an execution site.
How many strangers could circle the space while speaking of nostalgia
And of wolves in the hills? We find them
Thinking of nothing instead—there's no one to impersonate, nothing
To foresee. It's logical that prophesies would be emitted
Through the gaps left by previous things, or by the dead
Refusing conversation and contemplating beauty instead.
But isn't that the problem with beauty—that it's apt in retrospect
To seem preordained? The dawn birds are trilling
A new day—it has the psychical quality of "pastness" and they are trailing
It. The day breaks in an imperfectly continuous course
Of life. Sleep is immediate and memory nothing.

※

From sleep it's getting the elements I want, those
Not harried, not unclaimed
Not steam, not moderation
They minutely vary and stay the same
From waking I know that common names for a wind are echo, engine,
       and shadow
Memory is plasticene, farming protein, forgotten, and free
I have a board from a cave, it's the one with which I roofed it, a bluish
       gray but rosy and owlish adamant board, now a walkway
So off we go
No mention of mention but much of prediction and of musical time in
       wakefulness echoing
Musical time goes on
Sleep goes on what—on horses' buses and beetle chat

✳

Surely the sea for the deer browsing on the bluffs overlooking it belongs
With the sky
In the background of their beliefs (should they have them)
But for us adrift below with binoculars
We seem to draw it
Near and as nine pelicans fly
Low over the cast surface
North of the earth on which we're picnicking after wandering
Through the fog I remember
The zoo with its meandering veterinarian
Among the dreamy elephants (they won't charge—don't we
Wish!) swinging their trunks and the humidity
In the monkey house
While we live
We can notice such things
Not always to remember them well
Grey and swaying
Just as some people jiggle their feet or twirl
Locks of their hair or toss in bed
To alleviate anxiety in ever smaller increments
To repeat
Patterns over time to cover
Time
And again repeat
Just as a person might, working like crazy, day and night, to cover
The possibility that she isn't real
And won't get this work whose rules keep changing done
Without circumambulating the table on which it sits
Prowling in the purportedly relaxed but actually predatory
Manner assumed by cats
With intellectual momentum and psychological twists
That could be interpreted as prophetic
In retrospect far off and still to come
In the future towards which we're traveling faster
And faster in black
Then day again night again day
Again

Night the flapping of a black wing
Gaining velocity behind the jerking
Sun a streak of fire
The moon
A fainter fluctuating band over trees that grow, spread, shiver, and collapse
Mistily or dustily
Without a trace to my disappointment (I try to catch
Or create it) but everything's
Gone, whole histories
Like dreams sink into nothingness under
My eyes
There is a bakery—wow!—if I hurry
I can get rye bread and a dozen macaroons
And a blanket in Denmark
From a peasant painted by Pissarro
Who nursed the infant
Kierkegaard
At her good breast
Which she cupped in her strong pink green-veined purple-shadowed
        haystack-yellow hand and hitched
When he was done then stuffed
Back where it belonged without doing any good
Or harm
To her sense of justice
Poised on canvas
Spread to the wind

✽

Flagellate

        Gnomes in blue panties

     Hey, sister—don't squeeze

   Potential spinach-lover, lachrymose concert-goer

I like to stamp on corrugations

I've got to list that gum eraser

     Wild are the wildebeests, rapacious the masked
              raccoons that prowl at night

  Finish the list, patrol

     Gigantism
     Existence in space
     Quitclaim
     Humdinger
     Punk
     Buckwheat
     Individual volition
     Rub me with rose water
     Cast pearls before swine
     Get up steam
     Adieu, lambent flame of genius
     Fiddledeedee, spatula
     Rage, breathe, love-sick turtle-doves
     Bartending tiger, unthreaded Abigail
     Representative negative wood block Titian seascape
     Sink, o sun—noontide, shut up
     Waters of bitterness, come down the river
     Spaniel servility, pinned braggadocio
     Fire-eating, pot-walloping, post-feminist biker-chick

Solicitude
Fribble
Inquiry
Napkin and bushel and mañana
Give me a break—authenticity
Judge
Stammer
So please you

✳

some are nights
in which I'm told

Rain, queen

✻

I'd attributed entirety to the cattle—self-sufficient
solar calm from which nothing more was to be learned
in a bright place bellied by shade, one hemisphere
with the other implied where they might be twins
so gentle together, nothing more to be learned
since one can't be governed by superstitions
and omens are too incompletely informative

✳

One wouldn't say of something that moves from one place to another
that it's displaced. Take, for example, the backing beeping truck that I
can hear maneuvering in the dark like a big animal working its way out
of a thicket. To draw a perfect circle or triangle is out of a young child's
reach, but the resulting misshapen geometry in the drawing is all the
more expressive. If conscious thought can't make sense of this, then
one should let the unconscious try. The pastures, in spite of the rain
or perhaps because of it, are choked with brambles, an impediment to
travel, even of a few feet, but in late summer they are so rich with berries
that little travel (less than a foot) is required to obtain a feast. But the
skies are dark—all of them. Red and blue icing is spread along the top
of the cement garden wall and the thick railing of the stairs leading up
to the front door, but when anyone puts their tongue to it, they find
it disappointing, even disgusting. The unconscious mind can make a
whole of what the conscious mind knows to be disparate, disconnected,
diverse. This alone is reason enough to question the possible existence
of fate, the meaning of art, the existence of different temporalities, or
meaning itself. I lean into the wind, as if wanting to get a better look
at what's on the ground. The truck is driverless and to me, at least, it is
ineluctably abstract. I have no idea where it will go next; I have only the
vaguest idea how its engine works. I confess to being pleased with myself.
I look nice—slender, young, with dark hair attractively cut; it hangs just
below my ears. I've been out horseback riding for the first time in years.
I watch myself coming out of the bedroom, where I must have just been
looking at my image in the mirror. It is obvious that I feel gratified, good,
pleased at life. An internal conflict is not necessarily a mistake. It may be,
rather, evidence of pervasive, inescapable social and historical conflicts.
I can't extricate myself from them, but they aren't my fault. I've got some
carrots, broccoli florets, and bits of radish to feed to the horses. They
don't like the radishes. In 1977, out of a world total of 50,047 translations
of books, 19,577 were from English; the nearest competitors were Russian
(6771) and French (6054). Regardless of language, all seven girls in the
saga are identical, but this is the result of a technological inadequacy;
their creator couldn't draw and so he used found images of little girls as
his ever-replicable models, tracing them into his drawings. Regardless of
the diversity of their concerns, they come to them with only the one body.
Similarly, ideas are apt to conceal the suffering or pleasure sedimented in

them. I should mention monuments—they are always rooted in ideology. I can smell diesel, and the scent of mown hay. I notice a slight stirring of air. I don't forget to toss some carrots to the big, goofy dark brown horse. I don't like him very much and he keeps himself slightly apart from the others. The greedy black horse, mouth open exposing his big teeth, thrusts his head toward the broccoli in my hand. Out the window I can see a uniformly gray but not black sky, the color of dry cement. I hesitate to go into the office but I've every right to do so and so I enter, even though I'm feeling pressed for time and would have dreaded the now inevitable interruptions if I'd known they were going to occur. There are already six other people in the room, including someone on a table, legs up, undergoing a pelvic exam. Progress can delude us into thinking we are less vulnerable than in fact we are. As that thought occurs to me, Leo is given an injection into his testicles and he recoils slightly, says "ouch!" Thus nature reminds us of our unnaturalness and also of what we have done to nature. Then he's off the table, and even as I'm apologizing for intruding, he is gaily greeting me, holding a towel around his midriff but otherwise naked. There are seven of us, including a blond young woman named Cynthia or perhaps Melissa. Leo is our guide—a jovial and erudite native of the region. He tells us with enthusiasm about a certain monument that's situated somewhere in the surrounding mountains. It's called Magnagrito, but is known locally as Campe Proviso. It occupies a few acres, with extensive grounds, its gardens laid out geometrically. Cynthia—if that's her name; it might be Melissa—wants to set out immediately for Magnagrito, and she motions toward some high mountain peaks on the other side of town. There are bandits in the area and they've been known to snatch stragglers wandering along this path. Where now is Cynthia/Melissa? The landscape is green, rock-strewn, forested, mountainous. The sky is blue, the sun is pleasant. It's beautiful. This is Campe Proviso.

＊

I went to sleep in a pink hat and when I awoke I was sucking my gums
I telephoned my friend who lives in a crater and when she spoke I answered
I took out a loan as if it were a cow that I was moving to higher pasture and
        when winter came I climbed a pine tree

✳

Passion itself is not repetitious but it can result
in delirious reserves. The things said over and over are sensuous
signs of memory. But words say something more
each time and sustain our reputation and their real simplicities
are like bees drawn together while knowledge, that strong feeling
of pleasure, is best called a transition as it takes one thing to the next.

✻

I long to look like Audrey Hepburn under a big rain hat

✳

I wake
I wait to remember my dream which would be dull to anyone else
        but which could remind me of the stimulating day, the day
        that inspired it
There are details to that day I hadn't noticed during it
Something resulting in a rainbow or a ratio
An intransigence
Or logic

In the dream I sailed, stole, stalled, was jailed
My companion, a scientist, described his impressions and analyzed
        what we'd experienced much better than I could have done
I remember that an intricate corral held the shipboard animals
They were shaded by the dense and sturdy sails
Overhead birds which in real life would be called terns
        but there were called tongs passed over our embraces
We followed them with our binoculars, we identified them
        and characterized them as desperately casting Plato's shadows
An entire day went by
The circumstances remained under erotic analysis dreamed in self-defense
But that only means that the situation with its shifting expectations
        will begin again

❋

Dawn occurs and is varied
Dawn comes to bear, dawn coming to compose
Dawn is capricious casually
It isn't clarity that causes the sun to appear at break of day
It's the hour at which I most vividly dream that I hesitate
The dawn rhapsody is drawn up and out
The light sweeps the chill cliff I'm scaling
I can speak at dawn but at dawn the letters A through Z terrify me
Time was I wouldn't have slowly pondered but now I brush my knees
On the gray scale the light strengthens but I have never until now discerned a quantity of dawn
Dawn answers
The horizon faces, flushes
The cheats are ashamed, the prayers of prayers go on, procrastination must eventually come to an end
This dawn entails—it has implications and I am among them
Meanwhile, I'm fine and so is the weather
Now our undertaking begins
I come out from a misunderstanding and see the situation anew
Those who predicted rain have been proved wrong and are to be reprimanded by the light on the wall of the room in which I find myself
I'm up
The birds for song have the trees for perches
Dawn bushes and then there's an hour that is sometimes a small one and sometimes even smaller
And after a minute or two of this I rush but not far off

❋

Betrayal is a flimsy cruelty and an inflexible fantasy
Shame is a casualty betrayed by oversight

Real betrayal, free of calm, is only seemingly solitary
There has to be a premise for it, some communication

Accusation flaunts itself from its supposed view of reality
Reality is its defense and we are drawn like moths to it

We are incompletely lost in speculation, avoiding something to depict
How could there be no pin of blue, no shade of green, no grid of rapid
     tipping ants

Reality blows by and lives on prey and looks on sky and has now begun
How did the rice come rattling to the floor, what does the light at the
     window signify

✳

Perhaps my dear family can profit from my story
As it continues two pickpockets are denying a robust policeman's suggestion
        that they are 'suspiciously encumbered'
If encumbered, they insist, they would resemble kids with a lot to say
They would resemble unwanted sympathy
They would not be like holes in a hallway

✳

A straight rain is rare and doors have suspicions
and I hold that names begin histories
and that the last century was a cruel one. I am pretending
to be a truck in Mexico. I am a woman with a long neck and a good burden
and I waddle efficiently. Activity never sleeps and no tale of crumbling cliffs
can be a short one. I have to shift weight favorably. Happiness
can't be settled. I brush my left knee twice, my right once,
my left twice again and in that way advance. The alphabet
and the cello can represent horses but I can only pretend
to be a dog slurping pudding. After the 55 minutes it takes to finish
my legs tremble. All is forgiven. Yesterday is going the way of tomorrow
indirectly and the heat of the sun is inadequate at this depth. I see
the moon. The verbs ought and can lack infinity and somewhere
between 1957 when the heat of the dry sun naughtily struck me
and now when my secrets combine in the new order of cold rains
and night winds a lot has happened. Long phrases
are made up of short phrases that bear everything "in vain" or "all
in fun" "for your sake" and "step by step" precisely. I too can spring.

✻

O popularity, you are great in short-term memory
of memory easily fatigued. You are profligate
at using people's names, especially those of friends.
No bitterness. Our ancestors did it. The walls
of Troy are far away. Now to penetrate
the mind of a fictional heroine who will not look like me
I am driving to a city I won't bother to name housing
a disintegrating cardboard box, a rusting tricycle, clouds
thinly disguised as Pine and Main
and long stretches of capricious or sardonic behavior. And there is hurry
about it and I have a large refrigerator. In private
Pablito rolls a ball down the stairs between indifferent walls
under a slowing sun in diaspora
and in an Africa where pink's confused with white
that only becomes worse with time. Within I find him
playing solitaire. One-two-three-four: four stairs and the door.
Memorization—irreverent in spurts, passing strange, oblivious
to genre—gives him stamina, pleasure, power. It is only
because we've never forgotten
that we can well remember
some Alexander who is in love with some Dorabella.

❋

Connect

thunderpeal cunt with tell-all dick
        and
comedic cunt with short-term dick
        and
telepathic cunt with dallying dick
        and
critical cunt with equestrian dick
        and
kettle cunt with lickspittle dick
        and
syllabic cunt with canonical dick
        and
melancholy cunt with cartographic dick
        and
uncanny cunt with salubrious dick
        and
piñata cunt with butterfat dick
        and
oblong cunt with underwater dick
        and
subtotal cunt with mantelpiece dick
        and
fritillary cunt with cross-stitch dick

—and that is exactly what they did

✻

Perhaps you have what I was thinking? I said
Events *take* longer in *my* world, she said

.

❋

I could instruct the children to tree on all sides
of trunk planking, I could instruct them to screw up
their eyes and pencil their routes illegibly. Go.
Be almost indistinguishable, cross diameters, be
unwiped and stringy and political on pathways. Now
turn the page. Draw pilots. Be unsettled, be weedy.

❀

There was once a boy and he had a younger brother who was mournful
The older boy put a silver saddle on his horse one day and, mounting the
        horse, turned to the younger and said, "Sam, you've won"
A thief hidden behind a tree nearby overheard this and said to himself,
        "By tomorrow at this time it will be I who have won," but he was
        mistaken, as mournfulness cannot be acquired in a day

There was once a poor man who was hungry all the time
"How dare you? how dare you?" he shouted out the window to people
        hurrying to the shops on the street below
But experience of disappointment cannot be taught, and the people were
        deaf to his queries then just as they are now

There was once a sailor who had so many nicknames he no longer
        remembered what it was he should be properly called
He sat in the dark and gazed at the sea until his eyes ached and he
        wondered why the sea, which resembled an eye, never gazed
        back at him
But heroic efforts often fail, perhaps because emotion is often a poor
        teacher

There was once a princess who longed to be a cowboy but by virtue of her
        sex she was kept in the house without any shoes
"I'm no more dangerous than a mouse," she said one morning to the
        miller, who simply pointed to the baited mousetraps with which
        he protected the flour produced at his mill
Yes, restlessness is a characteristic of human existence and neither travel
        nor rapacity can exhaust it

There was once an astronomer who earned his living by promising glory
        to the king
On weekends he sat quietly with his daughter doing math—"efficiency,"
        he told her, "is best served by contemplation"
Now that was an excellent astronomer, and he is admired in pedagogical
        circles even today as a man who prepared for every lesson in
        advance

There was once a doctor who had a kind heart and long fingers and he
    lived by himself in a room over a bakery

"Everyone likes you plump and warm," the doctor would say to each of his
    patients, which was just what he heard the baker saying to his
    muffins as he took them from their tins
And so we see that to a reader in communication with a writer more and
    more information is made available—that doctor was a rogue!

Moral one: We are never the worse for our dreams, and a nightmare
    should not always be taken as a sign of a bad conscience
Moral two: Serenity can be achieved through fussiness (although
    probably only for the fussy)
Moral three: True justice is never abstract and should therefore not be
    blindfolded

That's what we can learn from these tales and from other tales too

✳

Ambivalence may be hidden in any act of kindness
Or every murky show of weakness thrown
Between giving and getting to the unforgiving
Whom one wants to know what one doesn't show
In one's dream diminishments
Of the fullness of life
From which one wakes with neither watch nor shoes
Shouting I've been robbed
Of sleep
Of which I've had way too little since childhood
Which was so long ago it might just as well have taken place
In a dream
Or between dreams
In a gap for which there's no evidence
From 7 to 9 pm on Wednesday, August 4
When we can get to know our neighbors at a block party
With local musicians and a police officer to discuss safety
Issues
There are measures
We can take
A little further
Down the beach armed
With briquettes after gathering driftwood
We can warm ourselves and warn others
Through the smoke
That with the wind off the desert will be driven toward Magadan
Where many worked harder than we are doing now
And died
Worse off than we are dying
Now
But every suffering
Is incomparable and unique
To the woman knowing what the weather was wailing
Over the dead
And specific
To the prisoner
Who knows that everything's misjudged

That's paraded through the universe
Behind men
Performing the cigar-smoking dance
Or the one about stalking
A panther or painter
Or women
Panting with invention
Since when one invents it is said that one's navel is attempting to leap
Off to another place
With laughter
Taking with it all the money it otherwise holds
Hidden just inside the entrance to the belly
Of life revealed as the curtain
That rises
Trails threads from its tattered hem
Over hams fat with layers
Of meaning extravagantly and elegantly but subversively and cruelly
                imitating
Contemporary personages
Whose self-appointed task is to piss
On every erect iris, purple violet, tripartite trillium, and tongue
Of fern growing under the ancient trees
Which though binoculars
May flatten them, provide bouncing habitats for nesting
Shocking birds as the cumulonimbus clouds darken
Deeply overhead
Forming pockets for all who have lovingly feared the light of day

✳

I am a tattered apology. I have two eyebrows
on. Give me wheels. Yes. This
is a big wheel. It's a fat one. That's
a lot of work for an apology to do.
It's a beautiful day. It's time for something.

✳

Just as the clock comes silently around to one
And another quiets the accusations that the hour lets fall
Like dull gray rocks down a cliff into the sea
I, an indecent (or maybe merely indecisive) passerby, guiltily hesitate
Or I, an emergency medical technician urged on by *Schadenfreude*, race
to the scene
Where I find another version of the I I am shrieking
At my children while brandishing the belt
That keeps my pants up, the black ones
That I spotted in a catalogue and ordered online
One night
Typically
I wake three times—i.e., thrice—each night
To worry
Typically
The worry precedes the thing
Or things or situation or event or character flaw or flaws or ominous
twinge or twinges
Et cetera
That I have come in time
To worry about
In this life that's life—entering time to worry—is it not
And there, just turning the corner—isn't that ... but
It can't be, she's dead, I think, though with just a few alterations
To just a few things
It would be she and she would be
Still alive
And finishing a task far ahead
Of the deadline
For sending dreams
Which are spells
Of attraction
In stride, with the right foot
Just swinging forward and hand up to knock
At the door late at night of the person I want to see
With seasonal flowers, a table cloth
And a platter of melons

That awaken nostalgia for wholeness
Which many people confuse with desire and from which many derive
Resentment from which in return they contrive
Their rationale
For retribution, vengeance, and fear of wild barbarians
Tapping at the windows, knocking
At the door to the kitchen, demanding
Dinner: roasted beet soup with crème fraîche
And champagne
If they're polite
Followed in the deepening dark
By Dungeness crab beside a simple butter
Lettuce salad
Peppered with arugula, nasturtia blossoms
And leaves, a baguette, cheese
And cold dry white wine
Poured playfully under the bridge
That every dinner table is
As we sit face to face, avoiding eye contact, having nothing to say, making up
Stories, remembering nothing
Of the day
Which imprecisely dawned
And should have been noticed then as it's invented
Now if not then as art
Answering to life as life
Answers art

❄

Sights flutter through the dark

That links

Example to explanation

That sets the plot

That wakes me up

Convinced that this stream of thought is carrying me

To someplace very bad

✳

We're as unlikely to escape context as weather
Without bubbles floating on the current and light
Reflected in the ripples and straws
Through which to breathe as we snorkel through
The undercurrents, torso supple, progress slow
As we detach ourselves or are perhaps suddenly separated
From our parents (if we are young) or children
(If we are old) like puppets
From their strings—which is more easily accomplished
Than the separating of avidly communicating people
From their dangling enthusiasms and eager affirmations
Fervently exhaled through the smoke from the meat on the barbecue
When the stocky dog, its coat a lovely patchwork, attacks
By turns vigorous, graceful, and grotesque
Weirdly, decoratively, viciously, and daintily leaving
Its 145 traces
Some no wider than a hairsbreadth and some an inch wide
Or wide as a man's thumb
As it presses the key and emits a C
In another octave
Of another caress
Unfolding
Unpredictably
As the lions roar in the adjacent bungalow with which we share a wall
They claw
Combinations
Which might just as well have been made on paper
With ink and allusions to Picasso's "Guernica," Goya's "Black Paintings,"
        or photographs from Abu
Gharaib (which spell-check can't tolerate and seeks to replace
With a gherkin, garlic, or Ghana)
But perpetrating humiliation and celebrating torture is a far cry
Glibly recording crying in resistance—resistance (resistance [resistance
        {resistance} resistance] resistance—Oh! nothing
Avails) rising, repeating—from ink and painting
I take up a Winsor
And Newton very fine sable (slash) synthetic

Brush and delicately even daintily but not girlishly dip it
Into Dr. Ph. Martin's # 25 Vermillion synchromatic transparent water color
And depict Mars
A grisly place
Under a bomb to which we go
Over again
To send over
Again and again
For recognition with burning
Eyes on film
From ruins under a bomb
Of happenstance held
There hidden lifting ruin
Buttocks burning maiden melting buttocks there bomb
Raised passerby lifted bomb sneezing ruins weather off the river
What river?
Every river
Weather taken
Off in mere disagreement
Largely lacking
History agreeing and soon forgotten
And nothing exploding but explosion
Closer to life than the shortfall of the ranging colonel's past life
That funds the dearth of creature life
Available for the local
Pet store parrots—
Parrots?
Yes, parodying parrots, toucans, lovebirds, finches, and green budgies
          dressed in silk
For lack of feathers
And disfigured, hot
Airlifted and remade in the cold
Of the fifty wars and fifty more with fifty sores and apple cores
And more and more
But the good news is that apple seeds do not contain
Arsenic, the bad
News is that apple seeds do contain cyanide
For processing
Apples (kind of)

Grinding and pressing
Against
The world you want to eat, they want to eat, we want to eat, I want to eat
Around them cautiously
As we might move through a minefield
Envying its treasure stones and anxious for the fate of our own
Bones having found their home
Inside our flesh and trusting to our skin
And wisdom on the march and pleasure
In our possessions as we puff and splurge, coming back
Full to bursting
We burst
In silence, under a cloud, heads in the air

✻

Optically riveted in a jamboree grievously fixed—oh!
Theft riveted
Things flung and things themselves seen in a spree
Go!
Things visible, things suddenly free
Photographs qualify
A crow!
A thing in redundant unexpectedness optimally driven faultily to know
   and quizzically found uncontrollable

✳

January 5. Nietzsche's autobiography. He regards himself as a vivid being and a "rule unto himself."

I compare this to "an intimate account of reality" as it's presented by "a schizophrenic girl." Progressively during her childhood she has "dimmed," as if fading in place. Her living has been immobilized by reality, monstrous and resplendent. Each detail around her has been too vivid to bear. Irritably, she writes, "Before they show themselves, objects should carefully consider what they are requiring their observers to consider."

Testing my own experience against these extremes, I remember that at an early age, I too distinguished myself from reality.

This is a common mistake.

Perhaps I didn't make it.

Reality was ubiquitous and yet certainly it seemed that only I, though still unknown, was real. I looked out as if from the only real vantage point at a world that was vague and banal and awaited me. Increasingly I expressed this perception. I wanted to be established.

In time, and paradoxically, my very willfulness diminished my singular, initial, original reality. Increasingly, then, what bothered—excited—me were the harder details; they were things—evidences—and they became impossible to resist. They existed, moreover, from innumerable points of view—they were expressing the will of the whole world.

And yet the will of the world was impossible to interpret; the possibilities were infinite. What did the world want?

I had always anticipated that it would someday want me.

One day I watched a bird land on the shingled roof of an ordinary house in our neighborhood and the house immediately burst into flame. Figures of smoke billowed at the windows. Dark blue fire shimmered against the pale sky. I heard someone inside screaming.

I knew that it was I who had shot a flaming arrow at the bird.

This violent conjunction of the imagination with reality—this moment of balance—was precise, effective, and irreversible.

A naked woman with wet hair ran from the house into the street.

✻

Sun!
    look ups

✳

A wet lynx or spotted rat grabbed a dog by misunderstanding it
Ants poured out

A jellied chicken ran across the floor
It burst the confines of the spongy grease on the kitchen sink

The cat was dead, its body stained by the dripping fruits
The windows shook

I wheeled under the inspector's gaze
But I made no complaint, taking pleasure even then

❄

What is this turbulent moment from which I can't detach myself
The great fact of thinking is dawn, but that's when I repeat myself
Before dissociation ends, the sunlight flares
Thoughts are leaping from a body that's a mere obstacle to it
Tragedy's wisdom gives way to comedy's heroics
What's left is an awful calm, and the laundry in its basket on the path
I can feel my chin become another person's chin
I watch the spoon as it rises, then I experience my hands, but who is using
      them?
There's no universe—the universal is an hallucinogen
What shared life offers is reality, but the only thing my perceptions of it
      provide are little bits of additional evidence
And though making sense of mute things is a normal thing for language to do,
      by unnecessarily elaborating the truth to make my story better than it
      is, I'm using language for defense
People say that's evidence of systematic cheating?
That's absurd!
I give my eyes to the horse and receive his in return to see out of

✻

The D baby
and her brother the D
toddler and their parents
the young D's came knocking at the door last night

The D
mother nursed the D
baby to sleep and the D
father remembered a book and fetched
a copy and presented it to me

The D
father and the D
mother left the D
baby in a small car with a bag of spoons

The toddler D looked
like a burglar in a dirty hat
with a miner's lamp
on his head—a head
no bigger than the button on the knob
that locks the door
onto the open windows of the second floor with an eye
to getting out that way
whatever the outside temperature may be—a figure warmish even
hot as a problem (D)
and then the stars appear after everyone
is too dead to hear them so they jump around
near the beginning
which continues to burn
at the door
though not one arrived at directly nor at the end
of a straight path that won't disappear
into the wholeness and interrelatedness of everything

Toddler D now
Boy D synonymous with a state of being dead

contemplates the transition through
the father's dream

      Girl D
considers the transition synonymous
with mortality into birth through the mother's dream

      Babies D move
in a frozen world home
to each old D in a moving world
no longer moving

✳

One night—it might be a moonless night of some year like 1873, the year in which cowboys are all wearing baby blue hats and long baby blue coats to match—some cowboys come galloping toward me over the horizon like bits of leaping, dust-raising embodied afternoon sky. They have broken away. They are as free of the sky as they are of the false idea of them we've received from old black and white photos. Their freedom is greater than what occurs during free association. Their freedom surpasses everything that occurs during a flirtation. The cloud of baby blue riders sweeps past me. Their freedom is greater than my airiest longings and yearnings and cloudy desires, which are less great than my rising sense of failure, of remorse, of spreading shame. The cowboys call over their shoulders, "Come to nothing," and the lullaby fades.

✳

a girl goes by riding a mulish bicycle in the ...

with a serenity that is just ...

        the opposite of ...

                worries die behind ...

                         it ...

        as behind ...

                           it ...

                             she goes ...

      clattering her chain ...
               which is at her ...

      source of contemplation ...

                         service solely as a ...

to pull
to be quite frank —

she races by

✽

Hideous forms—my legs—they kick. Out? In? Legs crawl out my skin, my brain has legs, my brain is legged. That's calm. Ten, seven, four, curious, on hill tops, machine-made, clutching their persons the symphony-goers run. The ill equestrians gallop forward, the horses delightfully clear the jumps. So many pauses occur. I want to be an orchid. Juanita slashes a green emotion across Napoleon's whip. My legs are tailing.

❀

to siphon of bison
        sister evince

        really

shit a phoenix

✳

Song giving way again
Every little narrative henceforth is in particular scientific
True, today the traveler goes from place to place at very high speeds
She goes in braids (nice touch)
She's given the requisite two weeks' notice but fired all the same: like a servant!

✼

A woman is expressing sympathy with a television character who is weeping and trapped, she is attempting to pommel and scratch her way through a grim inconsiderate crowd as the woman dolefully frowns. She leans forward slightly, it's an upsetting situation, but a woman *should* imitate the facial expressions of strangers in order to understand them though nothing's resolved even then, it's just a premonition of the feelings she's to have, as she has them, taken from the world, from a real actor, who has just shattered the windows of a new gray Honda sedan parked in the sun in order to get air to a gasping dog mournfully pressing itself against the door of the car on the driver's side.

Sympathy requires terrific optimism, bravado, and therefore paranoia. Already I regret having singled the woman out.

✻

A person may tempt but fail to keep sleep
    as insomnia wanders slowly in excitement
    from hour to hour
Sleep is an incipient
Inactive but not without confusion
    a person lies parallel to her sleep but not intact
This person is never independent
She is always present—or future with something to pursue
This person might claim—indeed she must: clothing, time, something pulling her
She enters her parable or fable, her lullaby, fantasy
She sleeps an insomniac lyric or somniloquy, she has a nightmare or incongruity
She dreams the shifts the scenes shift
She experiences drift or some equivalent, a transportation
You!
Think of the way the boat sinks into the obsidian pock like a lemon in ink
Imagine the dark dipper

✿

Into a carelessly careful confession details are thrown
Like short-lived exaltations we'll never understand
By a dreamer explaining a dream
To someone whose intentions are no good now and won't be better later
Unless things change and mules become fertile
But isn't it fine, says the forester to the farmer, to be weaned
From productivity—the accomplishment
And churning out—when by the heater on the floor
Lies the dog producing nothing
But shit
Says the child, it barks, it guards
Philosophy which turns
In turn
To gaze
Into the dog's gaze
As sad as stones
Or a sweater that a knitter leaves unfinished
At death for reasons that have nothing to do with the difficulty of the pattern
Which the child for whom it was intended chose
From a tattered book about a nurse who mounts a horse with enthusiasm
So strong that she overshoots the splendid saddle and falls
Into the sawdust surrounded by jugglers tossing bullets
And grapes as sweet as rock candy and as cold
As toes
So fat as to be offensive and wriggling
On their own without any sense
Of chronology
Which can after all only be recounted
Backward from the end (its
Tips) of the story
If time is to be credited
With supplying the logic required to bind
A truck hurtling through the night, weeds bending
In its wake to a dog lapping water
From a toilet or an erotic caress
To a mournful Marxist in a melodrama called Nell
Of the Navy dressed in a tight blue skirt

And a light blue sweater who's a gentle sort but with tricks
Up her sleeve
There's knife and a notebook and a comb
And a cell phone (you can call, the number's 6
91-5
91-0
1
26)
With some syncopation and knowledge of the secret
For avoiding sea sickness and bobbing
Without embarrassment, Sophia Loren says, "All that you see I owe
To spaghetti," emphasis mine

✻

    ipt

tup

        tra plaflundle

     na! flone ir

❋

And a hundred and fourteen guns
The guy from the "Nuclear Arts Movement" was kicked out on the very first day
He said ironically and I thought a little wistfully, O, very many
Till the sun rode high
He disappeared abruptly
Arms crossed over the stomach, hugging himself
Like a pistil after the petals go
The tree has a thousand tongues
And a snub-nosed revolver with the words
Weak flowers that are blown upon and bent
To roll up and down the windows of the blue-gray car
With such incredulity—wonder—mimicry—rejection—experiment—obsession
That all the things that are in us are
An encyclopedia, a common hunting ground for sexually curious girls
Finding ourselves robbed of our belongings
Snails, honeybees, and flies
And all the children of the dove-gray car pile onto the red vinyl seats

✳

   Temptations thronging through my hours are strong
and they launch a normal vocabulary
up and down and all around
"galloping, galloping, galloping, galloping"
   Disappointed, exhausted, and thrilled
as Gerard Depardieux playing Cyrano de Bergerac before falling asleep
to perceptual folding and disbelief in the sufficiency
of *that—that* life is—an utmost
with nothing to perceive
I put on speed, night following
like a flapping black wing
swooping me every minute over the sun and every minute making a day
I see
   Buildings rise and disappear like a puff of mist
as huge trees grow
up, delicate and fair, and fall away like dreams
of a bee sliding down the air
at the speed of an exceptionally languid snail
through which it tumbles into contexts—*episodes*—
as if everything were somehow more
than itself with the sun glaring off
the white stucco wall
as if praise were hard to give
   In cities
as full of people as history smart and telling
my quibble has been so chic of late that any repetition of it will seem
insincere
the first time and forever incomplete
as a holiday
but when I repeat
it the others get a look on their face
to indicate that these are a layperson's recastings of poorly communicated facts
involuted by the pressure of thought and worldview
that's not readily comprehensible
and easy to blame
taking its wild elaborations back into the dark

✻

       Papa is saying
Wee-wig, wee-wig
        Toddler is saying
Wig swenson dig der walloop
       Papa is saying
Hapkin hapkin hapkin
       As a sound unit
he must be
a very fine Papa
for he seems to muse on horsekind
or on horsekind's ineluctable musings
on humankind

✻

gender unstill

... damp and obscure

... becoming more so

       it appears to be something

             from those hollows swallows might be taken

they would start

         in admiration

                 with one strawberry
                 a baton
           curls
           merry voices
                with distance

yes, it is something
       though also an image
          of something
              which isn't the same thing
         that it is

✳

The clown cannot escape gravity; it cannot be light.

With its round paper-white baby face and enormously exaggerated facial features, the clown must appear to a child like a nightmarish caricature of the figure at which the child first smiled.

The clown is at once both newborn and a ruin. Gesticulating like a flailing infant but too big to be one, it is then the epitome of a senile being—and under its preposterous baggy pants perhaps a diapered one. We begin as small clowns and end as repulsive overgrown ones—perhaps this is the truth with which the clown frightens us.

The clown is a swollen prototypical human, its flopping inflated body a travesty of the rounded features of young creatures that we see as adorable, vulnerable, vivacious, which is to say "cute." It appears before us to taunt us for the inadequacy of our sentimentality, the limits of our generosity, and to deny us the narcissistic pleasure of nurturing tiny beings through which life has a future.

This goofy, looming, unpredictable, garish, frantic, bouncy, nonsensical parody of the child has emerged from beyond the horizon of childish optimism; it is clear from its expression that it has come forth out of despair to reproduce its own failure.

Like an adolescent, its feet are too big for it—as if it had yet to grow into them, but it never will. The only fate left to the clown is to accept its punishment, its humiliation, and then depart.

We laugh awkwardly and perhaps too loudly, as we identify with the clown.

❊

Walking around, posing, entering conversations, proposing
Events are staged
Carefully, artfully, tentatively, and relentlessly
Though the stage is a little one
In a theater maintained exclusively for magnificent premieres
Of consciousness
Whose adagios are long and always in the middle
While the allegros promising jollity telling lies all around feature virtuosic
        bits
Whose Caribbean, Basque, or Romany origins can be heard
In the striking of the clock
From which the cowboy drinks
A hurricane, the horse drinks from the lake a blue
That's gray or green and may be
Reproduced by mixing Dr. Ph. Martin's radiant concentrated Slate Blue (22B)
with his or her radiant concentrated Saddle Brown (13A)
But that's mere speculation
As I'm writing this
Pretending to be a filmmaker
Cinematically
Making things unfold
Not gradually but all at once like a letter
Folded
In thirds taken from an envelope and opened
In two seconds
Its message divulged: "your insurance premiums are going up" or "it's time
        to renew
Your membership in the NAACP" or "My name is Philip
And I am offering you an opportunity"
To which I will not wake
But stare
Disconsolately at the window or out
It at the blowing leaves on the light green tree
That cheers me
Up so I get up
And go
Into a room which is a robe

Left by an aerialist now on high in flesh-colored tights swinging and swaying
And swooping now back
To earth where her mask of being unmasked must be masked
Because she still looks naked
And feels it around the midriff and in her butt
On which she bounces back
Home again after a day at a circus—what a circus!

✳

Along the edge of the chapter Fredo's reading for fun Frankie stiltwalks his fingers stiffly, his fist like a Daddy longlegs' body is wobbling over the sill nightmarishly says Fredo flirtatiously oh.

✳

I found a wing today when walking
I remarked in pity, they cannot even keep their own names

No better than reason is the strut of a pigeon
The woods around it have it, it is theirs

Around a hill, through a valley, tinged with pity
One of my favorite things: wind in deciduous trees

Speaking of description: vulture aloft near the sea
No farther than the mountains is Pépé's bowl of water

Open to change—or don't
Dream—idea—personality comes on like a bull

The gulls pull at the air
Gulls in good weather, dark crow ducking

✻

I ran to pack my red suitcase, I knew that I was late
I couldn't find my underwear, I was held up at the gate
You left me in the waiting room and went on to Chicago
I stayed in France and drank red wine and woke as a virago

❀

Off in the distance just a minute ago we were going elsewhere
To see merchants on elephants said to be mischievous
As wind in the hay over secrets naughtily divulged
And dollars in markets soon fruitlessly spent
On wonderful books from which it's too late to learn
Anything memorable—that is, anything that *I* will remember
Facts having broken free and drifted off at will
And speedily from me though some come back
To my delight: they all look new
When they arrive—at least
I think they do surely
Something at least is out there in the dark
And light
Even if it's only bugs astride
Bucking molecules of water vapor
Rising from puddles (natural
Libations) leaping color from east to west with no promise
Of safe return
As when we watch the proud
Performers giving cues—a glance, a nod, a gesture
Without a break
The action changes and the twirling naked plates
Wobble like the courage of first-time lovers
And fall
With a roar from the ashen lions in a large white room
Leaping over a vase
Of white flowers, their petals
Now black
As laurel crowning clowns (those fast-paced characters)
Whose job it is to chatter over bones

❀

I mind this
Still
Though nothing at all
Comes
Now at the exit through which the voices come
Over
Algae then
Sand across
Grass into
House
One
Without closets
In tiles
And without
Water
And there's one that's tightened
And a vague one
With no place
And one
Among books
To stand on
The floor and piled
Into chairs along
With catalogues
From Legoshop.com, Sur La Table, Small Press Distribution, and Woolrich
And a black clog
Harboring a frog
But not a trace of it
Can I find come dawn
With drawing that pencil
Is a barrel
Of graphite
A barrel of organs
The body
Ordering in
The mind delivery
Devising

From the eye to its cave
Of an episode
Which will not give up
As it would take up
Otherwise spent
Its logic
Time that might be
The minutes more
Vows to spend
Worthily the hours more
Consciously the days more
Historically shared
Through windows
Overlooking—aha!
The nose (vestigial
Flare bestial
Vestige mundane
Iota vain)

✻

The Lost Pines Inn would be a good name for a motel, or No Sheep in the Meadow, The Lost Egos, The Downtown Country Inn, Mike and Ann's, Doug and Diane's, Bob and Joe's, or Just Joe's Hotel, Warm Toes Hotel, Anything Goes Inn, The Come Inn, The Company Retreat, The Hermit's Den, La Cave, The Little House Hotel, The Reliquary, The Happy Family Inn, The Rooster's Coop, The Corky Floor, The Henhouse Hotel, The Egg-in-a-Nest, The Rooks Retreat, The Cooks Inn, The Beat A Retreat, and a music group could call itself Crested Loader, or 10-Second Crossing, or 9 Car Train, or Thumb on the Space Bar, or The Unlike Minimums, The Shepherds Without Sheep, Sheep Without Sleep, Two Feminines, Autism, The Twice Maniacs, The Genetics, The Nasty Uncles, Interfering Women, but streets get named typically after numbers or trees or they're given the names of prominent as well as lesser-known citizens or the names of great cities of the world or the great letters of the alphabet from A to Z but in celebration of the things we consume the names of products and objects should be given to some streets (Tagliatelle Lane, Glue Stick Street, iPod Alley) and to encourage pursuit of intellectual professions a city's central thoroughfare might be called Mathematics Avenue, Neurochemistry Street, Jurisprudence Boulevard, or Lit Crit Street while at the edge of town the throughways and byways could commemorate abstractions and generalized conditions (as in Global Capital Street, Logic Throughway, Affluence Alley, Interruption Boulevard, Domination Interstate, Accumulation Highway) and another great name for a motel would be The Soporif's Inn, or The Archive, and Duke, High Spot, Drummer, Archimedes, Shadow, Ranger, and Gamelon might name some of the 220 horses at work under the hood of the blue 2003 220-horse power P.T. Cruiser that got me home by bedtime.

❋

I'm in a natural solitude—a spread—and I'm pleased
I've enjoyed social hauling and communal singing
Now I'm glad to withdraw from sound
"Now" *is* that withdrawal

❄

Ideas cross empty spaces in a game
We fill
As chickens fit
And thickets too
Or crickets on the banks across
The ice to eventuality, lamination, chrysanthemums, or size
Of cloud and grain
That's blown and something falls
Down the axis of ourselves, ideally upright, checking
The horizon but actually leaning
To see just what that is over there—some kind of flotsam
Though it might have been a head
Under worse circumstances
Into which we've installed
Our thought—an idea
Spontaneously repeating itself
With others without which we wouldn't be
Ourselves cutting loose
The ideology as it bobs, bends, and says nothing that our willfulness
        couldn't interpret rightly
Wrongly
Mounted on a sorrel rocking horse
Whose reins are made of braided hair
And whose saddle is slipping like a continental plate
Around a diamond
Because the girth is loose and we're bound
On a crash course so we're sure to meet
And then the rider will be thrown
Through no choice of her own
Into life as it will be
When it fails to accord with her ideas of what a county fair *should* be
—Timeless!
With barrel-racing for the cowgirls just outside
The barn in which the biggest sows suckle their pinkest piglets
Drawing crowds as large as those
Assembled for the judging of the chocolate fudge
Cakes, pickled peapods, needlepoint, loganberry jam, collective

Guilt and friendship quilts
For which there are neither synonyms nor antonyms
But there's cotton candy all around, I swear, Scout's honor
And no shit, I'll watch with utmost calm keeping
Camera up
And to my eye as the world shakes because it's interesting
That it is
The intensity of curiosity that flows, falters, follows
August with September, 11 with 12, salt
With pepper or salt
With sugar logically enough melting
In catastrophe and milk
To which a woman's crooning
Down
The aisle behind her cart mimics
A baby's squall
Or scrawl
Each squiggle re-interpretable and always adding
Up to what
We might term
A marvelous offset
E.g.
A mismatch becoming a rematch
Separating pugilists, then drawing them
Close, the one in blue
Shorts, the other flinging
A pashmina over her drawers
Showing her legs
Wearing green shoes
Over her toes tucked into socks
And the socking begins, one goes to the nose, one to the throat
Of a guy in the front row
With a digital camera that will never shoot
Thanks to the guy in the second row with the digital camera set
To receive and thereby gain
Impressions
Of a mummy! what sort of individual is that?

✱

Once there was a girl and she went for a walk by herself and came upon a hole in the ground no bigger than her finger. She sat down beside it to wait and watch so that she might see what went into it or came out.

Overhead large white clouds floated in the blue but they never obscured the sun and a spider crawled over her ankle. The clouds changed shape but didn't depart though a breeze was blowing, it carried a round brown leaf past the hole, then brought it back, and dropped it.

Why is that a round brown leaf instead of a brown round one, the girl wondered, just as she had wondered earlier why the large white clouds weren't white large ones.

Dissatisfaction with how one shapes one's thoughts is not the same as dissatisfaction with the shape of things, she said aloud and irritably, yanking at the nearest stalks of grass and pulling them out of the ground. Sulkily tossing them into the breeze, feeling sorry for herself but also thinking herself grandly or at least subtly intelligent, she failed to notice the shifting of the leaf over the hole and the ...

But whether it was a return or a departure, and of what, will be something we'll learn only tomorrow night, or some night not long after it.

First you must learn where the spider went.

❀

Thought takes position, position takes landscape, and there's no chance
Of rendering its eternity sans debris
And profligacy (some sort of soda) and rapacity (unjustly symbolized
By dogs
That cavort, then collapse
After eating their fill
Of beef-barley by-products and something resembling
Beans [precious miniatures])
In quest of heads
Of which the flowering weeds have many
Whose minds (hidden realities) we can't surmise
Nor surprise
If they experience irony
It's applied lightly
And only *as* light
From the sun, moon, or stars
Lapping time
Like cows nuzzling water from a ditch
Along the road among the weeds
Which are real
Facts in the making
We go
Out of position
To the zoo
To wonder what kind of social life is going on, how do people
Mingle if they do
Or find
Solitude, and what do they look at
Or see
Beyond the circulation of non-communicating autonomous human units,
        amorous or merely friendly
Couples passing black
Panthers, a birthday party of parents and 8-year olds in conical red
And silver hats passing (without noticing) the mountain
Gorillas, penguins, elephants, and retirees
And so forth or to the sofa to wonder
What is the world view on display

That we've overlooked
At an accelerating pace
Of pirates raising hair and curdling blood
Into cheese that would never appear
Maggot-rich in a market
Here since if it did the shoppers whirling through would shriek
And tend to linger
On the sill for the thrill of it—whatever
It is

✻

Philosophy should not be hostile to the eyes
The eyes project variety of character and possess laws of organization
        that defy rigidity
Philosophy is like the ear, its standard set to stillness, quiet
Every sound represents shaken forms
But every increment of time or space brings more light to the eyes
And this seems to be the source of the wild joy I feel now at being present
        and assertive

❀

gris

✹

Once there was a village surrounded by mountains and no one in the village could stand up for longer than one hour without laughing and falling down

Once there was a tiny black ant that scurried, paused, turned, scurried, turned, and paused again, and twice there was one and a third time, too, once, there was a tiny ant

Once there was a wayside weed that pleased those who saw it as it bent in the wind and bounded back again in the sunlight and died and came back as a frog whose singing lulled children to sleep until it was swallowed by a heron and came back as a strong and gentle horse that once hauled a wagon full of tired travelers over a mountain and later lived in a field without much grass where it died of starvation and came back as a musician who was very wise and very knowledgeable and could remember everything that had happened to him, including having been a wayside weed

Once there was a prince who liked to eat cherries and roll their pits around and around in his mouth, past his teeth and under his tongue and up again against his lips and sometimes from between them the pit would pop out and drop

✻

The water was rising, I got up on the bed
Still wearing the Hawaiian shirt he had on yesterday
He used his thoughts to draw a rudimentary circle on the wall
Hitting Beirut and killing 22 civilians
But now go the bells, and we are ready
Novelty is no better than repetition
That graces the walls of toilet stalls with hooey
And comparison with the dead—their slimy cruelty—and meatballs
Perched like ghostly birds
Believing in old men's lies, then too late unbelieving
There's rough life in the rust
Long-buried whore's eggs, razor-clams with shells
Pirates dressed in pink and pit-bulls on parade
With power to extend the longevity of learned fear in the mouse
And a heron on the horizon many sewing-days ago

Jane, Jane, ascend the stairs
Of the river's mouth at the year's turn
Thus predicting the shock to the tale that so entertains grown children
Of the animals that have nearly all forsaken us

❋

The pain is unrecognizable, located only

in the difference between visibility and its moral. You

and I will never have the difference right. Our

suspicions are too reasonable. But they're good

excuses—sporadic boundaries—the difference

between us.

Moral: The poised and luminous disparity between the stars is resolved
in their constellations, but the streaming associations which saw the first
pictures in them has frozen.

❀

While splitting a bagel and counting the minutes
In chatter so banal that every passion lies hidden in it
As we stand
Back (from the unicyclists, rowdy generals, and birdwatchers
Hurrying by) to back
With the people we love for love
Of their surreptitiously lost or slowly hidden histories
Secret even to ourselves from where we stand
Butter knife in hand and offering them jam
In its pot—they being the ones
We bought it for—fear gently removes us
Over time from the scene
But first we hear
Hard word of rocks or notes
Whose flights are musical and intellectual
But we aren't birds—we step
On things and stumble
Over them and cause harm to them or to ourselves
Or others, though mostly we don't mean to do so
In our blundering
The plundering is mostly inadvertent
But there's more to injustice than bad logic
And more to inadvertence than bad luck
Of the sort that plagues my boy
In dreams
He's lost
The tin box in which his colored pencils came
With which he fills
In distorted geometries and charts
Convoluted topographies
Through which he sets off mournfully
In a gray and green jacket whose zipper has colored teeth
Gnawing the air
Like the love one feels
Whose object is forever lost and cannot be

✤

The rain is banging on the ground
It fills the soldier's boots
It soaks the clothes he's standing in
And drowns the dog he shoots

✳

Today is "a day just like any other": the notion is at best mildly depressing, in some it could provoke anguish. Just to live—that seems like a desperate activity. It's a plight of some sort; to undertake it requires faith since it has no certain justification. In *Energy of Delusion*, Viktor Shklovsky comments that Tolstoy kept a diary all his life and in doing this he came to understand the human soul. Tolstoy repeatedly said in his diary that diaries were all one needed to read, people could find everything in them. For Tolstoy, "Napoleon" was just the name for an effect of innumerable, cumulative coincidences. Sailors of two centuries ago faced the sea without the naïveté with which we regard it today. They realized that it would be ludicrous to look there for individual or original ideas. A hush falls. Everyone falls asleep. Or there is a sudden knock at the door. We dread the ordinary. You go for a walk one quiet Sunday afternoon. You get mugged; the thief takes your wallet and keys, even your little notebook and favorite pen, the little tin of mints, the ticket stub, everything you were carrying. You are knocked down but not hurt. You go to the police who are or are not kind; they are not optimistic that you will ever see any of those things again. You go home and find the thief in your kitchen. That's a frightening prospect. But how did you get into the house if the thief has stolen your keys? You knock at your own door and it is opened by a thief. For days the weathervane on the neighbor's roof had been so steady that you'd come to think that it must be rusted in place, then it shudders slightly and swings, the metal quail turns to face northwest. Love comes through a void, a gap—not through gates but through the gateway, the empty space made by the opening of the gates, a pair of them, each swung back like a wing. From between those wings whatever could affect what becomes of you may come. Becoming a sailor, which not so long ago was one of the suitable careers for a middle-class young man wanting to distinguish himself and achieve social standing, has become déclassé: there are no longer any rich continents or mild islands for a sailor to discover; wars are no longer fought at sea (though engagements may be launched from sea) and, more important, wars fought on behalf of the bourgeoisie are no longer noble; ships have become floating factories. Rain, a million syllables. Perception is almost an end in itself. To make this more compelling, let's imagine that we've lost our bearings: it's dark and the flashlight's batteries are low. Every sound that by daylight provoked interest if we noticed it at all now provokes anxiety; we are on the threshold of fear. In pre-industrial times (which this dark hour resembles, though it's an arbitrarily engendered one), people shuddered in the face of the terrifying natural reality that surrounded them: the spirit-inhabited tree trunks, the lurking beasts, the miasmas out of which succubi might rise, the thunder. But now what's terrifying is the disappearance of natural reality, the realization that reality isn't real (it is only reified). We shudder now lest there is nothing left to shudder at. History can make even the happiest person miserable. But there should be some homosexual mating in it too; the performance thus far is, as they say, too hetero-normative. And so I find myself thinking of the scenes in *War and Peace* (the scenes before Nikolai Rostov loses a fortune, gambling with Dolokhov), when love is in the air. Everyone learns from stories, though not everyone learns the same things. *The Arabian Nights* is a story of stories, the hearing of which educates a ruler: once vile, murderous, bewildered, a slave to resentment (with its tendency to explain everything), he becomes benevolent, wise, confident, and suffused with a sense of well-being. It's spring; the skies are overcast, turbulent, with a pink glow to the south, a yellow flicker to the west, but the wise ruler shouldn't think his or her thoughts are free. The lower mammals (rodents, dogs, then cattle and sheep) are beginning to mate. Within days I see a pair of primates take up the game—they elongate, as if made of rubber. The source of the beauty of first their juxtaposition and then their coming together arises out of their previous absolute irrelevance to each other, like that of an almost translucent pink and yellow porcelain teacup and a dented hubcap. Yet they now ask for something more—shared knowledge of Italian, perhaps, but more likely an airplane. We can't see heaven from here because of the sky, our atmosphere—it's in the way. But there is some compensation: it's often blue. And I?—I'm feeling languid. What we call a ghost is a being that doesn't exist but looks and acts as if it did. I refuse to give in. I reject T, he rejects me. With a flourish, like a buccaneer tossing his cape aside as he reaches for his sword, he puts his hand on his heart and, retreating from my advances, he declares this to be "just too much social contact." It's almost impossible to dig into the densely matted soil under the vigorous redwood trees, but eventually we shovel off a layer of turf and there they are: large furry russet rodents in their burrows. They leap out and dart under the bed that I've just made up for our visitor in the car. He is wearing nothing but underpants, and with one finger he hooks the band at the back over his butt and pulls the pants away from his body, then lets them snap back. So it is that the cold trees endure winter, which is very hard. They try to sleep, they shiver. It is impossible to know what they are dreaming. But I know better than to attribute dreaming to members of the wonder-steady plant world. Nothing I or anyone else can do can live the life of the dead one for her; no one can take another's life for one's own nor give one's life to another. Love always contains a note of hopelessness. "We have the usual fender-benders and spin-outs during this wet morning commute," says the radio traffic reporter "at ten minutes before the hour" this dry, spring morning. "Get him a window!" I say out loud in response. There's a tale I like to hear told, it's called "Before, During, and After," though in books of tales it is sometimes called "Milk." Cross-references include "Diary" and "Dairy-maid" as well as "Eventuality" and "Weather." There are many passages in the tale that contribute nothing to the plot and seem inconsequential, but without them the tale would be nothing. Those passages are like the members of the audience in a theater, requisite but powerless to intervene. Nonetheless E reminds us that something must stand for elevated evanescent effervescent effluvial effort.

❀

The sea as it receives the changing sun is at all points
As agitated as a hound with fleas
The hound charges
At its tail
Its name is Sam and the sun
Above is like a dandelion
Just as it's blown
The course that each seed follows
We can't follow
Along the freeway
Cars race by carrying particular people (James and Ping, Kit
And Phil, Gyorgy, Carmen, Betty, Ishmael, Bunny
And Mark, etc.), each with a history
And fate—
Insofar as getting to their destination, parking, going in
(Entering is a major part of human life)
Can be said in retrospect to have been fateful—
That we'll never know
We go by, they go by, I go
By and you go
By whatever means are available and by the way
I have a green bike
That I'd be happy to give away as the tires wobble
When I ride badly southward at the end of the day
Which has already changed—it's beyond recognition—like a sheet
Of photosensitive paper too long exposed to an event

✹

The weave of the encyclopedic net from the sinking sun...

Of sunlight the volatile hibernation of many colors...

In the sky the wildlife a reservoir of deadly new diseases...

More violently more persistently more tormentedly a flower is my tooth

The mutilated relic, well, it's all experience, though it's a pity
Completion is accomplished in spite of everything

Somebody rose to be nobody's
And the Dutchman ate the others up

✻

pliers on eyes, stretching time, dividing pies

✻

Tony Parker cannot bear that the world on Monday assumes coherence, while for Nina Lee incoherence is what the world always offers.

❈

Wobbly deeds possess vitality in space
Wobbly deeds depart

      from mirrors in the sun

❃

In the certainty of seeing something looking
Thinks across
Sudden switches linked to leaving
Timed to the arrivals and departures of trains
Of messages
Bound to each other by a subject heading becoming less and less
Relevant to the contents of the chain of events around which the
messages clink
And clank in horror
Or shame at seeing
Maggots on meat
Or a mutilated boy
Objectively as if anything could be viewed as uncharged
In a milieu free of charges and with no one
In charge
As tugs labor from the harbor
Pushing barges bound for bargain
Basement warehouses
Home to contests without context mere spectacles
Interfering at eye
Level with reality my favorite thing
And all there is however
Sad
It's said to be
So here it is, so near and far
From acrid smoke and smitten dogs
And girls with basketballs and bugs
So small or swift they can't be seen in my myriad
Dreams of other things, jackpots and a woman whining
That she doesn't understand this proposition
Or "that is why they cannot be composite"
Because "objects make up the substance of the world"
At noon which will be along
Soon shucking corn
Past the orange house in which, fingers curled, the pumpkin people live
        long past the prime of life
But last

Like whales sipping plankton
From the Mediterranean Sea with rock fury
And rolling poetry that buoys a dinghy full of fisher folk pulling
In cod as the lighthouse beam passes like a hand
Of a clock
Rounding the bend that's a beacon for Evelyn—Evelyn—
Evelyn, have you legal experience—'til she can't stand it
Anymore
And she races out the door toward the Bering Strait
Legs crossing like scissors cutting an hour
From the journey and making it less
Gratifying than a bumpy ride in a wicker basket under a blue balloon
With three companions in search of the northern route
To the nutritious sun
As full of milk as the jug on my desk
From which my lamb whom I call To-the-Sky
Laps like the tide from sand or a child
From a cone
And beside it is my duck's egg and my rooster's comb
And a turd almost immobilized under the sofa
On which I set sail under a thousand eyes
From inside a rectangle no bigger than a grave
But it's a bed and its sheets are white and its blankets are red

✻

What is this argument worth?
Cold roast chicken on black bread, dear father
The best outcome doesn't yet exist and nature is as blind as justice

With my children in a rubber raft dodging larger trucklike craft
Pressed on by time, flight, and the rhythms
I call carelessly that the door is open
And the fields of buttercups flow and glitter

I was a journalist then adrift in the birth canal
Taking things in as passively as I might the plot of a drugstore novel

✳

I love says the acrobat
To read rarely passing
Even torn scraps on the street without stopping
To see what they have
To say I'm late
Or your car is
Blocking my driveway
If you don't move it
NOW I'll call
And have it towed, Jim
I'm sorry, I didn't mean what I said, I just thought
I did, we don't have, I need to get
1 lb ground beef, aluminum foil, briquettes
And corn unless it's shriveled, call
Turn left
Under the olive trees where we used to weed
And read
Or think to read
Since we must oversee our stories and not disparage those who tell those
        that begin
What a genius! I am
In my mother's room
And end ringing out
Ring out and ring
The fuller reason in
The kitchen where Mom is tossing
The kids
Are crossing
And Dad is washing
Westward, using his ears in the place of hands
To raise the sails that move the canoe out
Into the lake filling a pit made by a glacier
That Time itself was riding so
Slowly they say
Sometimes at night the moon rose and attacked
The very stones that the juggler cast over the hills and caught
On a scrap

Of music in a minor
Key tenderly pressed and audible
Still
It sadly repeats badly repeats gladly
Repeats
Facts
Falling like leaves
Lost from a book about deciduous trees
Whose black branches in winter cast grim shadows across the grand
      monument to history called Innocence
Or Ignorance
Perhaps—it's hard to say—the writing means nothing
Now to William T. Love and he means nothing
To me
But I admit and affirm that he had experiences and thought about them
Somehow holding his head
Around his ideas with his ears as pictures
Of the world held by the world
Marking its course
As something moving something
To something which cannot be any more
Infinite than all the sands that fall
Through egg timers and hour glasses
Shaped like pears, imperfect pearls
Or globs of dew on the leaves of a weed
That Pythagoras remembered
As himself
Becoming a bug, then frog, then someone
Now who's Pythagoras
Not me
Say
The equestrian in the park, the general in the jeep, the plumber under the
      sink, the actor
In a longish play
From which the thrill of political activism rings out
Rapidly ripples
Rotating clockwise for this is history
And so are the stars at least
For the astronomer and asters

For the botanist are something humans have seen
And savored and sown
In spots destructively
Devoured by the darlingest of goats
On precipitous slopes
For hire held
By shocking fencing
And fantasy shepherds
So like absentee landlords we all but expect
A probable leak from the slight smell of gas
And the dirty glass of the jugs of the juggler

✻

The demon of interpretation is riding
The same thick wood the day before
There were nymphs!
From them a strange odor of damp wool can never be completely
        banished
On sunny days a moment overcast
Apples I didn't pick upon some bough
To diminish the distance dividing men from birds
Crippled, illegitimate, deaf, unwanted
They are the chariots of freedom
In a kind of unstoppable commotion that passengers can't control
Through the thin frost, almost on separate stairs
Receiving one's own self from yesterday

※

Lost after all. You can leave any time
This rat's like me, she has a human soul
Too late: duty has become a habit, habit a duty
Poems distilled from other poems will probably pass away
But there's dance in the old dame yet
No doubt I have died myself ten thousand times before

✿

Once there was a day whose details stayed in brain
Nothing of its morning comes to mind though it might yet come to sleep
Well, don't we know it
Its beauty counts for nothing, I suppose
The concept of nature is merely compromised aesthetics
Sensual ethics far in bulk transcend it
So I didn't notice then but I notice now in retrospect that the peaches have
      displaced the kiwis near the market door
They call the stars to listen
Dry hands and cold shoulders, elastic bands, a fire siren, gun shots
There were once three girls, a strong one, a smart one, and a pretty one
They dreamed of love which came to mind and shuddered
It was not until the end that they finally could attend to it
Hi, there, Mrs. Oaks, the brawny butcher said
Where did you study to be a butcher
An entrepreneur never relents nor can a farmer be lazy
The education of a mind is built from continual substitutions
Constant change figures

✺

Leonardo da Vinci said about painting, *cosa mentale,*
the novelty of experience makes an unexpected "move"
and thereupon my heart is driven wild
and set off briskly for so slow a thing
at eight miles per hour on a road from one place to another
dirtily the dream an act of vengeance. It is not exactly
a life goal, a felicitous phrase span whose limits are vague
bellowing in bewildering variety up the front stairs
of the building pulling a gun, positive against negative.

✳

The mobile house goes down on tracks to the sea in the morning
This is where technology comes in
And it is the principle of best performance when lips are still
And the zoo at the end of Little Girl Lane
And the already dead future
And the seasons by air-conditioning
And houses where one cannot help but love
And another sort of smile
And not any more of either
The fingertips talk the animating contradictions
Nearer in fairy sea, nearer and farther
With barely time to pitch the tent in snow
And a bowl of peanuts, o voyeur

✻

and then and now and next to that
or sometime after Friday
and this one because of it
although that's afterward

—I mean this is after that
which was there when it happened
off to the left of the other one
on Thursday before that

✻

We are all being good sports, we are all disappointed. Word comes of a
suicide, and of a murder preceding it. Say there's a fight, a row, as between
L and M or B and J, the parties distrusting, disliking, and denouncing each
other: don't we call that an ugly mess with seals barking throughout the
night, individuals only occasionally identifiable in the din? And yet here
I am, humming like a shuttlecock as I move back and forth between the
sink and the stove, while a body—maybe more than one—is lying on the
floor, under fallen furniture. I'm going to set the place on fire, send it to
oblivion, and die in it. I'm wide awake and thinking that I'm dreaming that
I'm awake feeling curious about a dream—what does that mean, I wonder,
feeling frightened and ashamed. I like setting the alarm clock to go off at
odd, rather than even, minutes—say at 7:29 a.m. But reconciliation, should
it come, doesn't produce beauty. Wind begins to blow, torrents moving
in after we are safely home to overhear the occasional, meaningless and
ineffective brawl. I fell into a deep sleep and entered a dream, but of what?
I'm listening to the results of the Iowa caucuses which are not unlike the
reportage of sporting events with their talk of stamina, cheering supporters,
etc., varying the spacing, the timing, between words. At the margins of the
larger gaps, hang the individual words, isolated as if for later contemplation.
I lie on the floor, an image of Countee Cullen at hand, as the room, the
building, begins to plummet. The daring witness to a gruesome scene,
finding she can bear to look, cannot believe this to be as bad as things
get. Now I am thinking about the uselessness of umbrellas in a rainstorm
accompanied by wind. I imagine the first sensation of the flames, the pain,
and I crawl upward, as one climbs toward the highest point on a sinking
ship. Though I find round numbers unnerving, I gratefully grab two
soft cloths as if they were limbs of a beloved toy stuffed animal of some
indeterminate rumpled species and clutch them as the room tilts more and
more steeply and picks up momentum. Ugliness in art represents either a
failure to dominate or a refusal to do so. The vanity of those with smaller
handwriting means nothing, neither proof of modesty or insecurity, nor of
charming femininity or thrift. Indeed, this isn't so bad after all. People are
getting through whatever happened here despite their screams, which are
dying away, as are the tortured, who find peace in the end. The horror is
steadily diminished by the witnesses. Those awaiting torture are moved to
the attic where their tongues are removed. The immortal are already dead.
Better a slicker with a hood that can be tied tightly under the chin though it

makes a moon of one's face. I am ready to reroof a barn. It's as if femininity
has escaped the boundaries of the category to which conceptualization
tries to confine it (to the bodies of women and girls) to achieve a kind of
non-identity. My task is to put down a layer of what appear to be slices of
tomato. I come from the kitchen of a big house, where I've been helping
with the cooking. I'm looking down on a simple rectangular building with a
blue corrugated metal roof, the beam running lengthwise down the center
of the building. The pitch of the roof is fairly sharp. I'm only half awake and
thinking we should put a layer of tarpaper on the roof first, before laying
down the shingles, but I'm not sure how to attach the tarpaper to the metal.
Beauty, in life as in art, compels interest, then effort. I'm boosted up onto
the blue roof by a good-looking Spanish stranger. He is younger than I am
(he seems to be in his late 40s); he has longish thick dark hair streaked with
gray that curls behind his ears. He doesn't smile, he hardly acknowledges
me, he is simply there to lift me as one would a cat by the scruff of the
neck, grasping me by the collar. I'm thinking of a story carried in today's
San Francisco Chronicle about a man now miraculously recovering after
falling 47 stories to the ground when the scaffold on which he was working
gave way. The first row of shingles should go along the bottom edge of
the roof, but I don't see how to get to it without falling. The doctor says
that if you believe in miracles you can believe in this. Maybe there's some
sort of roofer's sling I could use. M is telling me that the house is leaking
in the wind-driven storm. A fear of heights in a dream represents a fear
of authority, either the king's or my own. My fall from authority would be
fatal, it would have happened and pertain permanently to an interminable
present. I wonder if I should be wearing roofer's boots, the kind with
a gooey ornate tread that can grip metal. With the ambivalence of the
triumphant, I am straddling the barn roof. I don't remember seeing any
windows in the walls, but there might be some. I am not looking at what
they would look out on. I am entering a bare room—there's no furniture,
no art on the yellow walls, just a tan wall-to-wall rough carpet on the
floor. On one wall, diagonally across the room from me, is a pair of glass
doors opening onto a garden. A white gauze curtain hangs over one of
the doors, which is open. Furtively A appears and then whacks a broom
against the edge of the open door. A scorpion! she declares. She misses
the scorpion and it shoots along the wall to the corner of the room, then
turns and comes straight toward me. I'm sitting on the floor. The scorpion
is squirming under my bare leg. It's under me, I say in a panic. Then it darts
into view and jumps onto my leg. It's going to bite, someone says—the

exact words I'm hearing are maybe "it's going to bite now." We live not to master the world but to be part of it. I pound my heel on the floor and the scorpion jumps off, goes a little way—it's pale yellow, delicate looking, almost translucent; it's about 3 or 4 inches long, with its tail quivering in excitement or anger and arched over its back. It turns and is charging toward me. I raise my foot, ready to squash it. I really do raise my foot and though that was eight months ago it seems as if it's happening right now. Rationally art addresses the irrational which it deems ethically superior to the administered world's (and its administering agents') rationality (dominance over nature), which is itself irrational and absurd. I am forging a fragile continuum, one tenuous juxtaposition at a time. I am recording a single sharp utterance by a large rough-coated gray dog. I am afraid I'll fall off the roof; the drop on one side is precipitous and long, the drop on the other even longer.

✳

Sleep can't put interpretation to rest, pigeons can't do *linguistic* tasks
at all. The woman pushes against an enormous door and she calls it *el
sueño*. Though neither complaisant nor vengeful, those outside seem as
indifferent as statues standing hot and melancholy on a sun-baked shore.
Logs will become cadavers, oaks ghosts, and there are circles that cruel
judges will close. It seems from her face that she is asking herself, "What
will happen next?" Then she puts in a potato and the soup overflows the
pot.

❋

Blessed is the stretch of the situated city that the rain rains on
In squares laid out like a checkerboard upon interpretation
And have simply to wonder and they begin to mean something
O spatula! O curtain rod! O railroad track! O Gregory Peck!
As if a table were a child able to respond the dishes are dumbstruck

✳

Those who speak about us today—how long will they talk
and then dream domes the high-rise, the sycamore, the child drinking
      milk
of sublunary things just because they seem ridiculous
at the hour of death, a whirlwind among breezes
as if to say now go figure out how all this was done
on thin tracing paper of someone whistling, another dropping
a spoon and this ice liberty

Tugging a letter from the beak of a sparrow
the crazy forest pulses and the gods strike matches by the millions
of words to stress, at whom to wink
the pushing sort of person who thrusts her way through crowds
very red in the face who was mopping his neck
when she might have been saying "Help me"

✻

o voyeur

    as stubble on haze
    and as dejeuner

✳

I am talking, caressing, crooning, but I can't calm the gaunt brown horse on the platform at the top of the tall wooden tower. It is lying on its side, thrashing (its legs are very long, the knees knobby) and writhing (its neck is long too and the expression on its face is one of total despair). It fights to get free, I am holding it around the neck, then I grab at its legs to keep it from throwing itself off the tower, but I am thinking that perhaps now I should let it go, as there's no consoling it.

✳

Guys! we need a password!

✻

I thought I saw my grandmother basting a baked ham
Then I saw it was two jazzy jellyfish setting up to jam
But when I speak of my "historical condition" it just means I'm feeling
bound to what has already happened, what will now never not have been.
What its significance is or was may remain to be determined, or it may be
deemed not to have any significance at all, to belong to the realm where
the answer to such narrative prompts as "so?' or "and then?" is silence.

✻

Written descriptions are no more than tickets to the game
And view my wasting skin
And love alone can lend you loyalty
Take the movement of the limbs and trunk
The tightrope walker's path is blocked
By chance one day, habitually thereafter
In blast-beruffled plume
It is here that a map would come in handy
A fright that only falling bombs could bring about
Of the sea coming, sea-like, in under the enemy
Fascinated by and afraid of the horses
At the annihilation of the enemy and of the enemy's memory
Alive enough to have the strength to kill
As a "good go-between" sees morning harden upon the wall

✻

Death is cast out of human thought by fear
Scolding squirrels in a tree

Make yourself up a cheering song of how

✻

Once there were seven clouds. They were quite distinct from each other and each bore its own rain, but all answered to the word "cloud."

But don't we share *words* rather than, or much more than, we share *worlds* (or even *this* world)?

This tale is about a very distant time and a very different place.

To understand something unfamiliar, it is often (though I won't say always) useful to compare it with something familiar. It is for this reason, for example, that you will find references in what follows to "people in cities."

Every tale, especially true ones, requires contrasts, just as every object, especially real ones, casts a shadow when the sun shines on it.

The eyes are like suns, or so people once believed. They thought that to look at something was to illuminate it. There's a certain sense to this—just as we can't look at the sun, so we cannot look into our own eyes.

At some distant time and place, spirits were present in everything. Generally invisible, they were nonetheless readily and ubiquitously perceived.

Then some Greek authority of 2000 years ago declared, "The great god Pan is dead."

But perhaps Pan simply went into hiding. It's not hard to find among the backwoodsmen of our time those who will maintain that trees have spirits, each one its own, though nowadays it's hard to find backwoodsmen. People in cities will often say that a specific house has its own particular personality.

When legendary heroes who have gone into hiding come out of it, which they often do (thus beginning their heroic phase), something terrible ensues (and the fall of the hero soon follows). This may be the reason humans are afraid of specters. Specters are always only half in hiding, they have always halfway reappeared.

Of the spirits in trees, or houses, etc., we may feel their presence particularly as a sensation that, somehow, they (the trees, houses, etc.) *care*—that they care about us.

It is terrible for them, and terrifying for us, that they should care but can't do anything to help us.

The seven different clouds with which this tale began now drifted over a backwoodsman who was standing alone in a clearing in a dense mountain forest. The superiority of his life to that of people in cities was as clear to him as the invisible air all around us and, though he didn't know why, he wished it to be clear to them, but he would have to put in an appearance to make it so, and in doing that he would cease to be a backwoodsman.

This quandary didn't keep the backwoodsman from acting for long, however. "Just for the time being," he said to himself.

His existence as a backwoodsman depended on his remaining in the backwoods, that much he acknowledged, but his existence as himself, with his idiosyncratic habits and unique set of experiences, his particular aspirations and the pleasure he took in watching the perpetual browsing and pecking of chickadees and jays, the unfurling of fern fronds, the flitting of wrens, and the swaying of weighty boughs waving twigs and leaves while weaving light and casting shadows high and low, these were worth knowing, and making them known depended on his being something in addition to, though not more than, and something other than a backwoodsman. He didn't know what that other might be, but he made himself a small canoe and headed toward the sea.

He knew he was near it when he saw a flock of gulls.

Gulls are among the least furtive of birds. They have nothing to hide, least of all themselves. They don't come out of the horizon, they fly parallel to it. They live in disorganized flocks, every bird for itself and every gull against all.

The backwoodsman in his imagination forgave them. In *Les Misérables* Victor Hugo, looking back on the Battle of Waterloo, writes, "Turenne was adored by his soldiers because he tolerated pillage; the permission to do wrong is part of kindness." It may be the wrong part of kindness, of course.

When the backwoodsman reached the sea it was mid-afternoon, the clouds had long since drifted away, and the sky above was clear. He saw in the distance an iridescent presence, a ghost horizon hovering between the still, translucent sky and the solid, moving sea.

In one version of this tale, the backwoodsman, struck with the immensity of desire, at this point throws himself into the sea.

He wants to be an artist. In every version of the tale, that's clear. If a child were tested on his or her comprehension of the tale, the right answer to the question "Why did the backwoodsman leave the forest for the city?" would be "He wanted to be an artist."

Art is the manifestation of peculiarly human desire; art is desire's embodiment, left desiring.

Birds, if they experience desire at all, desire differently from humans.

But even to imagine birds desiring is to indulge in anthropomorphosis, which is itself a symptom of desire. Or of dissatisfaction, restlessness. Anthropomorphosis is a product of boredom.

The backwoodsman did not leave the forest because he was bored.

Anthropomorphosis is at work in the human propensity to be afraid of specters. Furtive birds (wrens and rails, for example) have only one secret, themselves. That's what they dart into the bushes to hide.

Sea birds are almost never furtive; their environment precludes hiding. The thieves among them (certain gulls) are as bold as butter—but that analogy belongs to another tale. The backwoodsman can make his own way to the city; this tale is now about specters.

Specters know no justice. They receive none and thus have no knowledge of it. Sweet and sour tastes are also unknown to specters, as are sweet and fetid odors, although, with great passivity, it is said that some specters emit a fetid smell.

Specters do not emit gender and do not know it.

Specters do know pleasure and pain, but they experience them as indistinct from each other and do not know the difference between them. To some they are hellish, and to others they are blissful.

Just as sharks consider it natural and proper to devour seals, so humans regard specters: it is right that we should consume them, it is our right to do so.

But humans are often wrong about their rights.

Still, it may be true that when they are free the dead go to live on stars. It is said that on some stars only one dead lives, while on others there are many dead.

❀

Pipe me to pastures still and be
A message sent from one neuron to another
Irritable in an irritating room, perfectly-attuned
Like this slick and seeing ball

If sunlight strikes rock and the sea shines
It is oratorical, that is the bounce is so
And the second promise is slower still
And kept, bound to one eon from the next

✳

The imposing future will go past
Through some present
Moment observed or unobserved
Romantically calmly contemporaneously arbitrarily suddenly never
To be altered
Except in our knowledge of it
So the girl in the weeds
Offered war can stand by the door pounding
The pan in her hand—a loud round and large iron one
Taking everything in
Skin
Bare bones
Of beans, garlic, the zest
Of a lemon and the heads of one
Two or three
Fish from deep in the cold dark sea
Simmered in salt as thunder shakes the hills
Around the neglected garden that once produced flowers
And fruits that have faded
From a color called red to a color called mud
Or blood shrinking like dirty ice cubes in the sun
Rotting for the benefit of rats
Wasps, horses, cattle
And hermaphroditic worms living in the earth and eating
Tunnels in which to live and hide
As messages do when they are sent
From birds that hop hungrily, peck, chirp, and flit
About their business
So different from ours
In an avian economy bound to songs, seeds, twigs, grubs, bugs, et cetera,
          and eggs
Which are speckled, pink, blue, black—incredible
Aesthetic variety can be found
In eggs
Which women harbor too
As a bird enjoys its bird's-eye view
Of the self-combining whole be it

Another bird, the farms below, or a constellation
Known to some
As Tocolote ("The Thistle") or Annelida ("The Worm") down to the
    threshold
Then against the wall which rings
Differently, the pan is great
And resounds

✻

Go to the back of the class, Willie Roland. The central character is not Loretta Claire.

Alden Alfonzo and Eleanor McGee could easily pick some low-hanging green fruits. As they came off the branch into their palms they would ping like fresh water splashing into a metal bucket or smack like dice on a table.

Terence is feeling kind of tense and dishonest, and that's going to get in the way of our work. The clouds will precede us, soft as music, light as spray.

Every antagonist must be resigned to the enmity of the others. Tomorrow we can gather again in the white plastic bistro for a quick latte with laptop.

From the left comes a shout: You f-ing cultural pimps! Yes, we should have stayed in the laboratory yearning for data.

✿

The curtain is flapping—it slaps against the shaking
We are subject to the rule of metamorphosis. Somewhere there's a Douglas fir
pane of the open window. The cruel dialogue continues.
That is a carpenter with a pigeon soul. Symbols work.
That is a fisherman thinking he's tending his nets, a gecko
on the soul, true signs of the false or false signs.
They are butter and several camels. As duty is to beauty
of the true. What a negation! They are rose-stags! Goat-dahlias!
The weed through dew is to thinking: resolute!

❈

Solitude. The glow of decorative flickering
contents before an impenetrable mind. A note's
required, then two, congratulatory
or commiserating. Complete lack of progress.

✳

My shoes, my shoes—where are you?

❀

     While mice play in the sacks of wheat the backwater miller stands by his mill with his private face to the wind lost in worry. It may be possible to be thinking intensely but of nothing at all but this is not what the miller is doing.

     It begins to rain at 1:38 pm. A young man in dark brown pants and a buttercup yellow t-shirt runs past the drugstore, shouting things that add anxiety to the situation for some and zest for others.

     At 3:14 pm remarkable swirling currents of water are visible on the streets, and the little five-toed dancers emerging from ballet class at 3:35 shudder.

     At 8:11 pm the kleptomaniacal river carries off the smaller of two bridges, and with them an abandoned red car.

     Then it is midnight and the rain stops. Nonetheless there is tension in the air. Small dogs are barking.

     What the world has to offer is what millers have to suffer, and the next morning the miller will turn his face to the mill and set to work grinding the flour. But before then, he will sleep in order to release unconsciousness and let it flow.

✳

Notes before dawn in the spring
Of the year sound seven
To send with the summer a brazen
Unmelodious, peremptory, nagging, comical "week"
To wake
With many regrets
Like the cattle egrets that follow herds
From a tree whose name is standing terrain in the most bombed-out city
To be quoted here
Translated into human with wings milling
Like a child's mouth to a nipple
Whose name it has yet to speak
In the language of its mother and father and fantasies
With an egg more kissable than a lime
Of ideas between sounds rung from a bucket of authoritative metal
By slight of hand whose letters follow
And decline like the waning nouns
By the gray bridge where the whirling alders are
Like humans sticking to unperceived agreements

✼

Musical and efficient the sun
on Don Quixote's kids—several boys, several girls—mother
to scandalize mildly, though she was tired
of passing through the gloomy frame of history.

Leaves, like things, drop from a narrative, you, isolated
words, whistles, charm and console us
without ornament, illusion, conciliation, message, success
to jam the messages, to parody the songs.

When the sea gives grounds for optimism
we won't yet come to the abrupt end of the tale
able to draw a better duck the following day, a sharper star
with more shapely congruent arms.

Strangled by ten-fingered weeds or green with yellow rings
tin is the only thing that doesn't give in
and popcorn growing stale in the pale glow of the wisteria,
the jacket of an army uniform slung carelessly over a chair.

✻

A Naiad has plunged into a carnival tank, and I saw a bee
today pause, then soar, but where could she hide?
Well, life's explicit shine does sometimes blind us. Good!
Fenugreek—golden fenugreek!

✿

The past one-hundred years are not *just* a matter for infinite lamentation
    and impotent melancholy
They arrived trailed by a retinue of dancers and among them I saw myself
    become a wildly different creature
Out of my beds I went out of my mind and the world appeared in terms of
    it-seems-to-me
Alas, this precluded the unmasking of the hypocrite and left on the vine
    many boysenberries

Sure, pine trees became guitars, thus assuring that the past wasn't broken
    off entirely from the present
I can listen to music blowing steam over the blue band circling the lip of the
    cup
Let it come slowly up like a climber clambering up a precipitous cliff
Music, steam, and radiating dreams and pleasure I can't understand

The future is the time of care and that is why the dog shakes, because dogs
    are afraid of ghosts and thieves
The light comes and goes as in a psychoanalysis ten thousand years ago
    beside a fire in a cave
The future is the realm to which things return, fate and fauns, even police
    sirens and the birds that mimic them
I am waking with an eye to a future possibility, such as the warning bark of
    a dog, such as "smoke" emanating from a chimney in a cartoon
I am a bear among bears, a bird among birds, and a cattail

❋

Wild wind. Whoops. Sand the hat. The full century. Dry flags. Wow. Regional as driven bird twang on district vowels. Yikes. We've got a pulse. Not to mention the goats. The eternal train. Chat and clatter. Whoosh. A quarrel and it's over less than a dime. Some airborne pebbles. The salted map. Whew. Now waves, rain, torrent. And the gunfire is still to come. Disconcerting accents, durable music. It's the harmonica. Gosh.

✹

An elephant goes by, and then several lions—they are females: "a hunting pack."

Dibs canters by on her elegant bay horse—it has a lovely head and a powerful bearing.

As the horse canters down the road, the lions attack.

Someone throws a football to Dibs.

It appears anonymously but with an entry code: 38677; these add up but could not be derived by moving backward from 4.

The bay's legs appear to churn like a whirligig's blades.

It is tearing up the ground, an embroidered cloth spread over the branches of an oak tree, whose roots are the roof of the underworld, home to the afterliving, who know nothing of these lions, elephants, or Dibs here on the embroidered cloth.

A gazelle grazes nearby.

Moral: One shouldn't look too closely into the gaps in a story. They are hiding places, and what's in them is none of your business.

✽

In the spilling world sleeps a dog. Of narrow lines
the brotherhood and meats of carbon steel
of breath and theft and lentils rest
with girls in army tents. *That* is a guard, he said,
and *these* are the shops, Madame.

✻

We three are a trio in a tree
Where like airy riveters we are involuntary saints and all aghast
But maybe it's more punk than hip-hop to the cops
And when I want to say more, your tongue is in my mouth

Like news the day after an election a phalanx of Lipizzaners sidles past
Our praise and blame is left to alternate with praise in endless
        controversy
So let's go slumming on Park Avenue
And let's make faces when a member of the upper class goes by

Having stolen the last vestige of the past, the best of it
Idleness in modern life is a kind of deviation
That quasi-eternity in which the dead dissolve and fade away
And return, not without precedent

To what extent can I take back what I said following the uprising?
When just to have six tongues again new-found and wagging language
Out of a bicycle wheel, we can make a fan
From a broken chair, a parasol

✳

Roundup. C and D and A have the same
personal trainer and are getting strong. N
has multiple injuries from a fall. G glows
ever more roundly and around a kernel
of wild wheat names fall to the ground.

✳

    Though Sue doesn't notice it, she smells the damp dust, the elusive scent of the foxtails drying in the sun, and the odor of the sun itself as it floats gently back from the landscape on which it shines, as if its retreat (visible as steadily dimming reflections themselves little allegories of memory) had an odor but Sue doesn't really think so.

    Sue thinks through the night almost constantly of Sid, she thinks he's all but dead-to-her.

    Sue says to Drew my son rarely thinks of me at all.

    Drew says Sid's maybe through with that for the time being, he is after all now a young Marine.

    No, my hopes are lost, says Sue, then why not, says Drew, your fears.

    Momentarily Sue with relief understands Drew, she relaxes, but sometime during the middle of the night, she'll wake and worry anew.

✣

This might be the supine blue end-whistle, the substitute sword of soft gray rubber. It's all inaugural in a poor climate. The old women walk in rashes. Another word for them will come at some other more sinuous stretch of time when the straightening of rows has become impossible. Then nature will enjoy the good joke that the desert tells the thunder, the one that the trees with ears will overhear and shiver to. Golfers beware. A good person must take his or her self seriously and tell it the truth about itself. It bears some resemblance to an apple and some to a turtle. But it should be reassessed nightly and reassigned as necessary to maintain its state of preparedness. If only it could take dictation from gravel. The boy with the soft rubber sword is obliged to it for a vocabulary of fearless speech which includes those words and the prototypes for others in the serious game of matching the self to its intentions at a pace that's instantaneous. This has all to be accomplished by the scurry at the end-whistle when it's all over the field. It's that kind of all-over, as in perambulation or the application of color.

❈

There are many parts to any mechanism
and Sigmund Freud is buying carrots. Then the uncertainty
of being useful is the decisive factor
amid the fallen leaves. They are brown and roughly curled
things and events get memorized, then memorialized this way
but in differences keyed to incompatible views of the one event or several
in a year. Late daylight on the street climbs out from under the trees
into furbelows and curls and again pretends to listen, waiting for the
        moment to leave
with the enemies of music who are so sadly missing melody
which is continual it seems to us and lawyers, players, plumbers.

❊

To achieve reality (where objects thrive on people's passions), enormous effort
and continuous social interactions are required, and I can't get started
without you. Not here—over there's a better place to begin a funny story.
History with its dead all shot through with regularities in the woods
and following what looks like a cow-path
is part of a creature's sexual magic. Its recorded words
now are just a small memento meant to trigger memories
which will give us energy when the right time comes.
Every afternoon high in a tree
the forest vagabond naps while time hangs
like a swarm of midges, trembling on. It might be female
but it has a phallus's tendency to jump up. How lonely it is
to think that I can only think what I think even while he is thinking—our
          thinking
just our respective working body's hum. And while the warlords of Mycenae
          were storming
Troy the foundations of their own societies were crumbling, too.

✿

your brain is like a lake
being splashed by rain
sleep, little baby, sleep
the droplets spin and spread

your mind is like a web
being blown by wind
sleep, little baby, sleep
someone's at home in your head

✳

Sedants among the pedants sit. The crystal gazers spin. I've got blisters.

❋

I am a failed fire chief
I am a failed thief

Didn't I fail at the wrong thing, aren't I a failure at failure

Failure is inevitable
I am a fan of failure
I am a failure flailed by failure
I leap into failure
I relish the self-pity that's produced by the self-loathing that comes as a
    consequence of failure

The sauce has curdled, the meat is tough, the custard is runny—the meal
    is a failure

Failure is the offshoot of argument—but then failure occurs too from a
    lack of it
Moral failure
Financial failure
Social failure
Heart failure, liver failure
Failure to thrive

Failure is familiar
I'm faking failure, I'm reconciled to failure
Failure has a certain allure
I'm quick at failure
I'm clumsy at failure

It's said that girls are failed males
There's been many a worse failure

Failure clings like gum to the shoe
I set about forging failure

Fuck failure

I fit failure, or failure fits me
A guy fails and is pursued by that failure
One could succeed and thereby fail
Every painter fails, every parent fails
I failed to dot an i
I failed by failing to tell a failure that he'd failed
Honesty fails
Dishonesty fails
The unprincipled fail without principle, the principled fail to excess
There are whole classes of failure, genres of failure

I'll risk failure
Courting favor, I'll court failure
I failed geology, I failed Greek, I failed to show up when expected on
     Wednesday
Memory fails
Flags fail
Luck fails
Curs snarl at the failed
Families bury the failed

Fail farther, fail fatter, fail in a particular field of endeavor
Failure is succinct and sucks sugar
Failure figures

I am a failed detective, a failed botanist, a failed equestrian
I am a failed mariner
I am an errant failure

So, this is what happens to failures!
Failure

✻

Our thoughts wander, and, except when making an effort to remember, we hardly notice any friction.

Remembering takes no effort in sleep. We slide into it just as we slide into forgetting.

The affinities with which one disperses in dreams and which enable one to be everyone in them shouldn't be confused with waking kindness.

In dreams, one's large identity is all memory, peopled but with something other than rapport. It's waking life that rapports populate.

There is no empty sleep, of course—no sleep without content—but sleep says nothing—it has made its break.

Nothing done in sleep can be said to count; numeration (sequence) is not part of sleeping strategy—it's all one.

Or it's all none. In sleeping we go backward toward the true blank, where it's been permanently though prematurely installed.

It's precisely in sleep that we come to things installed, things in endless summation.

Sleep maintains records but doesn't record. That is wakefulness's passion.

Sleep balances by flowing. In order to keep its balance, it never stops. Even awake, we sleep.

We know, of course, that nights belong to time, whose dark divisions exist as if to harbor sleep so that it can take place at the edge of life and make a place for dreams.

Dreams themselves, though full of gaps, slip things into the gaps that harbor the indivisibility of the middle zone of life, where indeterminacy and intermediacy are so easily confused.

✳

crystal butter—
      there's a clatter to puzzle!

from the frowning couch
      my queries stray into some rhyme room
            as if that could save the situation

never in a million rocks
      will the sun square
            as if that could situate a slat

✻

But...

✻

But...

✻

a ghost and I can't sleep
together tame

nothing comes of nothing
thrust on me

✿

The waking state can be termed the true yellow cling peach of romance
In a word, anatomy
It will return as a harmless subject inhabited by all
Neighborhood: abandoned former battlefield
Social structure: artsy/inefficacious
Favorite leisure pastime: whining/watching rented movies
And the May month flaps its glad green leaves like wings
They have been put in alphabetical order like a piece of ice on a hot stove
If it is a wild tune, throw away punctuation
Never reject anything, nothing has been proved
Go back into the city to find that lost serenity, as I wake from it

✻

This tale like many others happened once and only once and I will tell it only once and then no more so listen well and if you do you will understand why I have filled my basket with sand.

There is a small cottage halfway up a hill not far from a tree from which early one morning a prince fell from a sparrow's nest when he was still so young that he didn't know the difference between shadows and reality nor remember how or why or when he had become a sparrow and he never would, since no one can remember anything until they have lived for awhile and when one is old reality has cast so many shadows memory goes blind. This is why the history of the world depends on tales, which are like potatoes and the sky at night and have many eyes.

On this particular morning four beautiful girls had come out of the cottage to play and when the prince saw them he leapt into the air and landed on a branch in the sunlight. The girls' parents loved them dearly and had dressed them in brightly colored shirts and told them to beware of cats which in this part of the world are the size of cars and it is only because the cats are forced to wear bells on their collars that they haven't devoured every living thing for if they had you would not be here to hear this tale and I wouldn't be here to tell it.

Now listen well and if you do you will understand why it brings good luck to dream of a silver bucket in a yellow cart.

"We will name you Chip," said the youngest of the girls to the prince, "and bring you dishtowels to sleep on."

"We will bring you seeds to eat," said the oldest, "and also some raspberries."

"We will build you a fortress of sticks," said the younger of the middle girls, "and it will be your house."

"We will fetch water fresh from a faucet for you to drink," said the older of the middle girls, and now I will tell you their names since if you know those you will have a picture of each to see with your own two eyes and you will understand how it was that Chip the sparrow prince fell in love with all four. They were named Martha and Florinda and Alicia and Clair and they each hurried off to do as they had promised but when they returned Chip was nowhere to be seen.

Immediately Martha realized that no good book tells the same story every time it is read.

Alicia looked along first the south side of the cottage and then the east for the prince, and she saw some daisies and some ants and a caterpillar and a red doll's shoe. Florinda ran to the cottage's north side where the weeds and ferns grew in the shade and she saw some snails and a dented toy truck and a stone that because it was damp was blue. No one saw any sign of Chip.

Clair looked up into the sky and said, "Actually, I think Chip was a star."

'No way," said Martha, and she scattered the seeds she'd collected onto the path near the dish of water that Florinda had filled from a green garden hose coiled under a faucet near the back door of the cottage. Clair placed a folded dishtowel onto the ground under a tree beside the path and together the girls arranged some branches and cardboard over it. They set some raspberries among the branches.

That is the tale, and if you have listened well, you will understand that the four girls lived happily ever after.

✿

sleep awhile o bloom o baby
     like a spider on a table
don't be dizzy, lift a ladle
     sweep the moonlit tiles o baby

sleep awhile o bloom o baby
     like a thistle in a meadow
don't be restless, catch a shadow
     keep from windblown dunes o baby

sleep awhile o bloom o baby
     like an answer to a riddle
don't be furtive, clutch a pebble
     deep are spoon-fed dreams o baby

sleep in excess

no access

✻

She had it in mind to go up the fir tree to watch the nude
pigeons, or angels if transparent, or a flea, like a man in mental
wind churning in the creek, two men on the road bouncing by on
glass with the greatest pleasure but not until then able to say,
it's on the floor. I am a laconic and I have a truck. My statuette
not then and cannot now do better than a tree trunk or a wrist.

Then a terrible noise, impossible to mute, from the proliferating
swimmers in the pool, should they come, watching herself
(described by workers who've been in on it) swelling in the heat—
the scrapbookist! or scrapbookessa!—a woman in the balance
though in a bad place and rolling fresh raw leaves—arched
horses splashing dust, passing moodily as milk down the trunk
of the tree—but none of it could affect her integrity.

❉

Suddenly a film
Weathering a film
Shareably a film, shakily a film
A film about a man who's framed
Action!
A film on ranching, a film on fishing, and a film on throwing rocks
A film and its soundtrack
A woman in a film who will be in none to come
A film about a woman good with guns
A film of some influence on the history of film
A film that features female stars now deemed angelic, earthy, funny,
        foreign, or forgotten
A film rarely seen
A film of a spiraling plane in flames
In a film on mountain-climbing there's a voice-over, in a film on la belle
        époque there are stills
Only a film
Lastly a film
We film still

❋

The animals were descried and described
because to us they're all very much the same
and wind again, waking us afraid
and testing freedom through the weeds, white
walls, messages taken
cum grano salis from stem to stem
and moon floating, barriers
flying all around—a circle of superior souls

Then I wept to show my concern, my virtue
and yams
and ghosts in the voice of a wintry consternation
and over the field at the end of a fantasy
like a sentence in a language coming from the throat
I came home to the zoo and the many animals that lie there oppressed
where sunlight falls to the ground

I'm left with an impression of previous things
which are learned by drawing the characters over and over again
on the continuous slopes of mathematical ferns
so rapidly ascended and descended by the bumbling human gait
as to alarm me and leave me
without psychological insight, contemplating a cantaloupe
churned by the undertow's counter-flow
though its ripostes, comments, shouts, screams are mute
against this form of rationality

❋

            it's beginning
and a gift ball of blue glass
and a photo of a brother
an altruistic perseveration
a drawing
a drowning
an excursus with pedagogical intent
a cautious child
a wrinkle
a wind
a single cell in a uterus
and audible content
a long lullabye
a hieroglyph
a glue stick

and it continues
            a marmalade
            an eventuality

and fades

❉

Hunting drives me to happiness
Now I am speedily proceeding, though with no sure goal
Life is forwarded
The wave of it begins, a wake of fantasies and flaws
Reacting quickly I write this

Light like an avian predator travels downward
It casts seemingly causeless impressions of other things happening
Shadows
Fractures
Trenches, gullies, burrows
Valleys
Or troughs between waves torn by cormorants
The ice cracks

I don't forget that facts can sweep the imagination—the waiting that is
        slowly produced by everything that matters
And when everything that could be real is, then all that can come to be
        are fissures for sentiment to fill
All could happen in a sudden tranquil pull

Hunting moves but happiness is motionless
Between two moments a crash occurs, a stone sinks
Mouth goes to neck
Things that I know are now my bounding sights

This is the opposite of an elegy, mourning what's found
A round of ideas discovered by their opposites
They are in sentimental circulation and it is as such that we accomplish
        them
Their whole purpose is to cross
And the very notion of an intersection is scenic
There the I of which I speak is not I but its coincidence

I is that which moves across its life
I am scratching, chewing, poking, and whispering into my surroundings

The hunting directly follows what I see
It is an exciting fact that we are sad because we weep, afraid because we
        run
My desires tempt the knowledge I hunt
Experience flees and makes dreams probable

✳

I travel with my cathartic animal who follows with the emotional abandon of an automated lamb, its footsteps hissing behind me on the gravel road. I have stored my executions in wicker baskets lined with flowered damask. Who am I?

✳

I have lived aboard a ship stranded by a terrific immobilizing wind.
Now it is Thursday and I'm to teach a class at a technical institute—I'm
to lecture on Noh plays. M has loaned me representative masks, L has
volunteered to come to the class and sing, C with dramatic compassion
has sent seven e-messages of encouragement. Just as I step into the
driveway, I'm arrested. My long-postponed life of crime is brought to an
end before it has even begun. B has achieved enormous prestige—will he
use it to help me? Dawn brings all speculation to an end.

Index of titles and first lines or phrases:

Lyn Hejinian is the author of over twenty volumes of poetry and critical prose. She has also engaged in a range of collaborative projects as well. Most recent of these are *The Wide Road* (an erotic picaresque novella written with Carla Harryman, which was published in 2010 by Belladonna) and *The Grand Piano: An Experiment in Collective Autobiography* (a ten-volume project published between 2006-2010, co-authored by ten of the original Bay Area Language writers). Hejinian teaches in the English Department at the University of California, Berkeley.

The Book of A Thousand Eyes
by Lyn Hejinian

Cover text set in Castellar Std and Warnock Pro.
Interior text set in Warnock Pro.

Cover art by Chaffee Earl Hall Jr,
"untitled collage," 1967.
Courtesy of Lyn Hejinian

Cover and interior design by Cassandra Smith

Omnidawn Publishing
Richmond, California
2012

Ken Keegan & Rusty Morrison, Co-Publishers & Senior Editors
Cassandra Smith, Poetry Editor & Book Designer
Gillian Hamel, Poetry Editor & OmniVerse Managing Editor
Sara Mumolo, Poetry Editor & OmniVerse New-Work Editor
Peter Burghardt, Poetry Editor & Bookstore Outreach Manager
Jared Alford, Facebook Editor
Juliana Paslay, Bookstore Outreach & Features Writer
Turner Canty, Features Writer
Craig Santos Perez, Media Consultant